I DON'T NEED AN ACTING CLASS

I DON'T NEED AN ACTING CLASS

MILTON JUSTICE

APPLAUSE
THEATRE & CINEMA BOOKS

Guilford, Connecticut

APPLAUSE
THEATRE & CINEMA BOOKS

An imprint of Globe Pequot, the trade division of
The Rowman & Littlefield Publishing Group, Inc.
4501 Forbes Blvd., Ste. 200
Lanham, MD 20706
www.rowman.com

Distributed by NATIONAL BOOK NETWORK

Grateful acknowledgment is made to Tom Oppenheim and the Stella Adler Center for the
Arts for permission to include a letter dated July 10, 1980, from Stella Adler to Milton
Justice. Used by permission.

British Library Cataloguing in Publication Information available

Library of Congress Cataloging-in-Publication Data

Names: Justice, Milton, author.
Title: I don't need an acting class / Milton Justice.
Description: Guilford, Connecticut : Applause, [2021] | Includes index.
Identifiers: LCCN 2021019379 (print) | LCCN 2021019380 (ebook) | ISBN
    9781493061259 (paperback) | ISBN 9781493061266 (ebook)
Subjects: LCSH: Acting.
Classification: LCC PN2061 .J87 2021 (print) | LCC PN2061 (ebook) |
    DDC 792.02/8—dc23
LC record available at https://lccn.loc.gov/2021019379
LC ebook record available at https://lccn.loc.gov/2021019380

Contents

Preface

I Don't Need an Acting Class

Acting is no mystery. If you have a craft, it opens up this mysterious thing called talent.

—STELLA ADLER

You cannot discuss acting without someone listing chapter and verse the names of actors who have had really successful careers, and "they never studied." Based on the misconception that acting has to do with being "natural," it seems as if this could not be a difficult task. I don't think it helps that the most commonly asked question an actor gets is, "How do you remember all those lines?" The implication being that all it takes to act is to memorize the lines and say them *naturally*. Ah, if only that were true! I'm also thinking early childhood success contributes to this idea. I must take this opportunity to mention that in the eleventh grade I won Best Actor in the Dallas, Texas High School Play Competition for my performance as Estragon in our forty-minute version of *Waiting for Godot*. Let's face it, if I can win an acting prize doing a Samuel Beckett play at the age of sixteen, what could I possibly get out of an acting class! It's a shock to the system to find out there is actually a craft.

My former student, Ben Robson, a British actor who is currently co-starring in the American television series *Animal Kingdom*, told me that he felt as if all he did in the first year of drama school was take notes. He added that the amount of information was so overwhelming that he had no idea how to use it all. Learning to act is a bit like the story of the centipede who was doing just fine with his walking ability until someone pointed out that each leg was doing something different. The centipede became so obsessed with what each leg was doing, he could no longer walk at all.

So why then would someone who has the knack for acting tempt fate by studying what they are apparently doing naturally? And there is no question, you have to have a knack for acting. Not just anyone can do it. A fact: You both have to have the knack and you have to work your ass off. The author David Grove commented once on an actor who had been a big deal when he was in his twenties and then sort of dwindled into obscurity. "When you're born with natural ability, there's a tendency to get by on that. But it's like a well; when it's dry, there's nothing left, because you've never worked to build that foundation."

That really says it. When you're not clear what your process is, you have no idea why you were so brilliant the last time. Or worse, you don't know why you sucked. It's like starting out on a trip without a map or a GPS. You're dependent on a blind hope that the inspiration of the moment will tell you how to get where you want to go.

It is true that there are some amazing people who get a great part and, through working with the right people or through keen powers of observation, they develop a craft without attending a class. Many years ago, I got a call from my agent asking me if I would meet with a client, a writer-director who had sold a movie and had cast an actor who had never had an acting class. I was asked to watch the actor's screen test and give the director an opinion about whether to enroll the actor in an acting class during the three months before shooting began. I watched this extraordinary young actor in a couple of scenes and knew immediately the answer. No! He should definitely not take classes in the months before the movie began shooting. His impulses were extraordinary, and you don't want to mess with them. That actor was Ryan Gosling. Ryan Gosling would get his actor training by working. What he has is an amazing actor instinct, which he has had the good fortune to learn how to access and control through on-the-job training.

Even Ryan Gosling's ability is limited, however. When asked about his process, he said that he looks at the part and dials up or dials down parts of himself to access the character. As fascinating as he may be as a person, he will always be limited by who he is. Should he ever be asked to play a uniquely different character, he will somehow pull the part down to a variation of himself. It's not what we call acting.

The decision to take acting classes boils down to this: on the off chance you don't land a series of career-making parts, it's probably a good idea to learn what you're doing and continue progressing to do it better. The director David Fincher quoted some wisdom his father passed on to him: "Learn your craft—it will never stop you from being a genius."

Some Introductory Notes—Stella Adler and Constantin Stanislavsky

There are very few theater people who would argue the fact that Constantin Stanislavsky is the father/mother/god of the study of acting. With the advent of *realism* in the late 1800s (Ibsen, Strindberg, Chekhov), acting was forced to change. No longer were there good guys and bad guys on stage— there were human beings. Stanislavsky would be the first actor/director to dig deep in the search for a road into the process of acting in this new form. He spent forty years studying/directing/teaching the artform and, in fact, was in rehearsals when he died. Of interest, he was also living under house arrest and members of the Moscow Art Theatre would come to his apartment to rehearse. (The Soviet Union considered Stanislavsky extremely controversial, but he was too well known a world figure to send him to prison in Siberia, so he was confined at home under house arrest.)

I have the unique honor of being an acting teacher. I've been teaching since the mid-1980s and have had the great joy of working with countless actors, many of whom have enjoyed extremely enviable careers. My own teacher was the legendary Stella Adler. Among her students were Marlon Brando and Robert De Niro.

The first words Stella Adler said to Constantin Stanislavsky were, "You've made me hate acting." Stanislavsky's response was to invite Stella to come to his flat the next afternoon (they were in Paris) where Stella would take her first acting class with the master. I think of this as an early indicator that even Miss Adler knew she needed to study. They spent the next six weeks working every afternoon. She would be the only acting teacher in America who studied privately with Stanislavsky. I like to think I'm two degrees of separation from Stanislavsky.

Their beginning work was fascinating. Stella reported that the first thing Stanislavsky said to her was, "Tell me where you have failed." They discussed at length what the issues were and what had caused her failure. He then told her where he had failed (Dr. Stockman in *Enemy of the People*). What a lesson to realize the beginning of learning can come from solving your failures. The important follow-up to this is, think how much you have to know in order realize why you failed. Actors will throw out, "I sucked" or "I nailed it" as a description of an audition or a performance, but unless you can follow with what was wrong—or what worked—it's a useless indulgence.

The Moscow Art Theatre first appeared in New York in 1923. Never in the West had Americans seen such consistently brilliant acting. It would change the entire approach to actor education in this country. Many of the Russian actors stayed in New York, teaching and influencing countless actors in an ever-growing American theater movement. In 1931 Harold Clurman, Cheryl Crawford, and Lee Strasberg organized a collective of actors, influenced heavily by the work of Stanislavsky. They called themselves the Group Theatre. They would become the first important theater movement in America.

Stella's problem with Stanislavsky came from the Group's actor training, under the leadership of Strasberg, who insisted on the use of emotional recall as an essential element of their classes. Stella had a violent reaction to this and blamed Stanislavsky's teaching methodology on her misery. The private study with Stanislavsky not only assured her he had abandoned his early work with emotional recall—he opened up entirely new areas of the actor process.

Stella Adler returned to America, completely contradicting the early interpretations of Stanislavsky. Elia Kazan once admitted, "When Stella Adler brought back the phrase 'given circumstances' from her time with Stanislavsky, it influenced my entire career." What given circumstances made clear was that a character's actions, as well as the drama in the play, came from an *inability to cope* with what was going on in the circumstances of the play.

Stella Adler was a passionate devotee of Stanislavsky and she eventually opened a school, passing on to her students both what she learned from him and her adaptations of his work. I was extremely fortunate to be in class with Stella for five years and, like so many who studied with her, I would drop in regularly for a recharge—the sort of thing normal people do when they go to church. Her mentorship would last for almost fifteen years. In the mid-1980s, she asked me to teach for her and eventually made me artistic director of her Los Angeles theater company.

When Stella Adler went to study with Constantin Stanislavsky, she took with her a secretary who made notes. "Stella asks." "Stanislavsky answers." The notes were lost at some point and, of course, there was only one copy. If only Stanislavsky and Stella could have emailed each other.

This book is a collection of emails between me and several dozen actors as we explore various aspects of the technique of acting and the disparate problems actors have with them. Some of the emails are direct questions actors have sent me, others are reflections from work in class and in rehearsals. And periodically I bitch about performances I've seen and what I think was missing. It's also based on thirty thousand hours of work with hundreds of actors through the past thirty-some-odd years.

Acknowledgments

I would like to thank my agent, Kevin Huvane. I can't resist. It's one of those things I've always wanted to say. Kevin is Managing Director and Partner at Creative Artists Agency (CAA), and he's been part of my professional life since the mid-1980s. It never occurred to him that I would write a book, but when I told him I had, he immediately hooked me up with Mollie Glick in CAA's New York office. Mollie got me to Applause Books, where I had always hoped to be published.

The first people to slog their way through an early draft of this book were my former colleague John Vansteen and my fellow Grace Choral Society member Susan Knopf. There was so much book in that first draft, I'm in awe they made it through. Both of them were enormously encouraging and gave me great advice. As did my writer friend, Mark Donnelly, who suffered through countless emails with the subject heading: "Does this paragraph make sense?"

My best friends in college—Jack, John, Tim, Garland, Kathy, Sally, McLure, Greg, Sharon, Chip—were all obsessed with the theater, which made my early theater days very productive. All I had to do was climb on the prom float with them. Because none of us came from a theater background, we were forced to learn from each other. Each other's mistakes and insights, I should say. My early jobs, assisting Gerald Freedman, John Morris, and later Lee Grant, opened me up to a professional world that cared about theater as a creative collaboration. And my friend Margo Martindale, who was in the first play I directed, challenged me to step up my game.

When I met Stella Adler in the summer of 1976, my entire sense of theater changed. She was the embodiment of the nobility of studying an artform and I longed to be a part of it. I was like the newly converted. I moved immediately to New York and began what would be an extraordinary fifteen years of studying and learning from a true master. I accidentally slipped into teaching because my friend, Grant Show, was auditioning for a play and he was looking for some help. Suddenly there was the opportunity for me to pass on to someone else what I'd been learning in Stella's classes. I found a place where I belonged. After an amusing disagreement with Stella about what would eventually happen to the Gentleman Caller in *Glass Menagerie*, she pointedly announced, "I want you to teach for me."

I have been extremely fortunate along the way with my many co-conspirators, who've allowed me to try and fail . . . and try again . . . and succeed . . . and then fail again and . . . Well, I think it's what we call a life in the theater. Tim and Bonnie, Ruffalo and Thornton, Kenny, Anthony, Kristina, Thor, Joanne, Susan, May . . . all of these incredible people who gave me permission to grow and learn when I first started teaching. I also owe a debt of gratitude to Deb Margolin, who unrelentingly questioned me about my understanding of acting concepts as I drove her to Yale for a semester—and to Sharon Carnicke, one of my most cherished colleagues. I owe them all.

The idea for this book came from a series of email exchanges that began in about 2007. I like email. It feels like I'm having a conversation with one of my students, or a class, or the cast of a play. Corresponding through email forced careful, cogent writing and communicating. Not that all of the emails in my book are overly thought-out or complete. I consider the study of acting always to be a work in progress. It's a journey that I've had the great privilege of sharing with countless actors. But for the present, thank you: Abel, Akende, Alex, Blake, Cameron, Chris, David, Edward, Erika, Evan, Garrett, Giancarlo, Grant, Greg, James, Jay, Jean, Jenna, Jesse, JP, Justin, Justine, Kaleb, Karim, Kevin, Kyra, Mark, Maia, Marie, Matt, Mel, Michelle, Mo,

Noah, Nick, Paul, Peter, Raphaël, Robin, Teddy, Teo, Theresa, Tim, Tony, Victoria, Walker, Wesley . . . the many, many actors who have dug into this work with me and struggled to find an answer to the overwhelming question: what does it take to become an actor?

1

Some Fundamentals

Sylvester Stallone—The New Brando

Some thoughts as we enter our first class.

Having a specific relationship to every aspect of the world of your play is essential to acting. Quite simply you must be connected to everything you talk about. When you're not, it sounds like a grocery list. And if what you're talking about means nothing to you, it will mean nothing to the audience and they'll nod off. Or, in the case of many a production I've seen, you hope you can nod off. Quite simply, you must be connected to everything you're talking about.

In November of 1976 on the occasion of the opening of the film *Rocky* there was a half-page headline on the front page of some New York paper.

SYLVESTER

STALLONE

The New

Brando

We might look back in horror at the idea that someone could think this might be possible, but Stallone's performance in *Rocky* blew people away. At the time this headline appeared, I was one of the producers of what would become one of Tennessee Williams' few Broadway flops, *Vieux Carre*. While riding in a taxi with Mr. Williams on the way to a rehearsal, with that raspy Southern accent of his, Tennessee asked me, "You know that new Italian boy? Stallone?" Of course I did. He continued, "I'm thinking of letting him have the rights to do a new *Streetcar*."

Sylvester Stallone as Stanley Kowalski?!? If someone were to suggest something like that today, it would seem ludicrous, but at the time we had only seen Stallone in one film, *Rocky*—and we loved him in it. Obviously, Tennessee did.

The idea of Sylvester Stallone as "the new Brando" defines a great truth in acting: *an audience responds to an actor's connection to the world of the play.* The audience feels what the character feels.

If the character is in love, the audience should be in love. If a character is outraged at the injustices of capitalism, then the audience should be as well. If the character is being crippled by his family pressure, then the audience must feel the same. Sylvester Stallone's Rocky had a passionate connection to everything about the world he portrayed in *Rocky*. He was connected to the plot, the relationship to his girlfriend, the city of Philadelphia, and certainly with his character's passion for boxing. All of it. And it was not some intellectual connection—Stallone's soul was connected to Rocky Balboa and Rocky Balboa's world.

The necessity of being connected is true for every play, every film, every television show. When an actress playing Nora in Ibsen's *A Doll's House* really understands, connects, and brings to life Nora's problems, the audience will be unsettled because they will know what it's like to be a woman who is only living for her husband and children—and not for herself. It is powerful for an audience because they see and understand the problems of a human being called Nora. The power of the play comes from the actor's connection to what the playwright is trying to say.

So where do we go wrong? The lack of connection—the lack of experiencing—starts very early in the actor's process. It starts the second an actor answers a question about a play in a dead tone. And I'm talking about any question or comments about a play. The title. The author. Where the play takes place. Who you are. What you want. Absolutely anything connected to a play and the actor's process that sounds dead fights against acting. Acting is not about answering a question correctly. "I see a door" has the possibility of either deadening you with its accuracy—or bringing you to life because of a specific relationship to it.

> QUESTION: *What's the name of your play?*
>
> ACTOR: (think of that dead tone, as if the actor is answering the question while texting) *Long Day's Journey into Night.*
>
> QUESTION: *What's it about?*
>
> ACTOR: (monotone—as if reading out loud the answer on a freshman theater literature exam) *It's about the day Edmund finds out he has consumption and his mother descends into a morphine stupor.*

Good for you. You've answered all the questions correctly. Now you can act the part.

I blame it not just on our educational system for making us believe the key to everything comes from having the right answer, but also on acting teachers who tell you there are five questions (or is it six?) you need to answer in order to play a character. And actors answer the questions and think they own the part. Or, even worse . . . Mandy told me a teacher demanded the actors in her class write "three single-spaced" pages on their character. When I complained about this, Kaleb responded, "Don't let the MFAs at the universities hear you. It was required to have a three-page minimum Character Analysis for every role I played."

All of this dead answering questions and dead reporting of the facts is what makes acting dead. It's the reason I stopped Peter the other day when he walked on stage and I asked him why he was coming into the room. It was as if he were giving us the blow-by-blow description of the process of walking into a room.

Reporting the facts of a play is destined to bring a deadness to acting.

When Stella Adler said, "Your talent is in your choices," she was giving a key that allows our choices to ignite our talent. But merely making a kick-ass choice is pointless if we don't sense your relationship to it. A teacher I met in Prague told me he would say to his students, "Mean it!"

Something happens to you when you connect. You feel it. You get that thing in your body that says, "Yeah! Got it!" This will carry into all your work, whether you're building New York in the 1950s or the Salisbury Plain in *King Lear*. When you're preparing an audition and you make a choice that thrills you, it gives you an edge. It makes you want to go to the audition. The confidence in your choice then resonates. Not only does it give you confidence, but an audience responds to your connection.

Mr. Stallone's passionate connection to Rocky Balboa, like Julia Roberts' connection to Erin Brockovich, is a lesson for us. It's not outside looking in. It's right in there and we as an audience get to share the experience.

The Biggest Sin

Talent without a technique is like a Porsche without gas.

Where do actor problems start? Hence, the question: what is the actor's biggest sin?

Dear Robin,

I'm convinced that this sin is so big it was given to Moses and emblazoned on the tablet with the Ten Commandments, but it fell off as he made his way down Mt. Sinai. An essential commandment of acting: *Thou shalt not make performance decisions when you first read a script.* This sin rears its ugly head constantly. I know it's a struggle to read a piece of text and not rush to a performance choice, but I would love for you to move slower and really consider the nature of the facts of the play.

I understand the problem. It's almost an automatic response. You read a piece of text and immediately decide how to perform it. Or as JP mentioned in a session last night, "They want you off book, so the first thing I do is worry about memorizing the lines." This automatic response doesn't just make you come up with a line reading; you make instant decisions about the character, the character trait, and quite possibly their mental state. Without really being aware, you are saying there's only one way to say a line and only one type of person that would say those words and they have to be in a certain mood to say them. And I would add to this sin the idea that your conclusions are no doubt based on what *you* would do in this circumstance, not what the character would do in the given circumstance of this particular play. The fallout from this is almost irreversible. Once you make these decisions, they're really cemented in your interpretation of the part.

Falling into this trap is the actor's biggest sin.

Noah got stuck in class yesterday, because he couldn't get where he wanted, even though he *"heard the performance in my head."* The impossible task he set for himself was trying to duplicate something he had in his mind. Not only had he heard it in his head, he'd rehearsed it mentally. The consequences of this is that you end up doing a kind of a bastard version of a performance you've imagined. And, because Noah had heard one particular section as extremely intense, he muscled it.

I would add to this sin the idea that not only do you have a performance in your mind, if you've leapt to decisions, it's very easy to have the wrong performance in your mind. There is probably not an actor alive who hasn't read a line of dialogue and immediately decided how to play it. This is rampant in TV and movie scripts. So much of the dialogue is meant to sound "real," which means it leaves you open to playing a cliché, meaning your performance becomes a cliché. You read a line of dialogue like, "I hate you" and you immediately know how to play it. It doesn't even occur to you that it might be something totally different.

Another danger is that we not only jump to conclusions, we begin to make other choices based on this knee-jerk reaction. Teo did it the other day. He was working on a monologue where he is telling his brother what an asshole their deceased father was and for some reason he decided he'd told his brother this piece of information hundreds of times. I'm not even sure where he got that idea, since nothing in the text gave any indication this might be true. But, this need we have to make performance decisions as quickly as possible allows us to jump to anything, as if making a choice, no matter what it is, is somehow a key to good acting.

I Know Nothing

Dear JP,

Every play will have a slightly different road in. Certain facts will hit you on your first reading and, while it's important to honor your first impulses, you don't want to make assumptions without really looking in depth at what a fact might mean. The danger is that you will miss opportunities for talented acting choices. Merely assuming you know what something means without exploring it in depth kills your acting and sends you plummeting into making clichéd and uneducated choices.

Yesterday I was coaching Maia on a monologue from the play *Detroit*. From the moment she started the monologue, she was very tense and muscled. It was one of those moments you often see with actors, when you are much more aware of the performance than you are of what they're talking about.

The character was a drug addict and Maia had jumped too quickly to make a decision on how you play a drug addict. Matt made a similar mistake last week with an audition for a television series. He grabbed on to one line of dialogue and decided the scene was a seduction instead of a confessional. Both Maia and Matt are good, solid actors. But they both made immediate decisions about how to perform the text from one reading and it sent them down the wrong road with a vengeance.

I was having dinner at Joe Allen's with a former student, who shared the opinion: "The best thing you ever taught me was, 'Start every play as if you know nothing.'" Coincidently I heard from another former student a couple days later. Garrett was working on a film, playing a guy who was head over heels in love with a girl and he told me, "I approached the part as if I had never been in love before." The point here is that although the first impulse might be absolutely dead on, even starting by saying, "That's one possibility. There must be others," allows you to wander around the other elements of the script and see what choices open up to you. You have unlimited possibilities. Years ago, I took Robert McKee's weekend story structure seminar. He adamantly insisted, "Your first choices comes from a place clamped on the side of your brain where every cliché you've ever encountered from every television show you've ever watched lives."

I'm always amused by the difference between what we do in "real life" and what happens in our acting. In the real world if someone asks you what it was like to live in New York, you can talk their heads off for an hour. But if my play takes place in New York, I make an immediate decision, based on the premise, "I live in New York, so I know what that means," and I move on to my next fact. We miss so much because we don't stop and consider the many possibilities that exist in terms of actor choices. It's why I've always thought it's easier to start as if you know nothing. It forces you to address any facts of the play with a fresh eye. If my play takes place in the late 1800s in Sweden, I have no choice but to start from scratch, so everything feeds me.

Another deadly consequence of reading a play and deciding the performance too fast is that we make the play about "how I would respond if it were me." In the scene between Sarah and Mandy in the Donald Margulies play *Time Stands Still*, Jenna leapt to the decision that she hated uneducated people like Mandy, so she did the scene like a total bitch. I have a feeling it was based on a personal distaste Jenna has for people who are not particularly sophisticated. But it was not even close to the right choice—and it made Jenna's character completely unattractive. Mr. Marguiles gives us a huge issue to explore—the morality of war photographers who film catastrophes and don't participate in helping those in need. It's impossible to make your point clear if you condescend to your partner and talk down to her as if she's a stupid idiot.

Akende can almost be forgiven for his sin, as it's practically shoved in your face by the writer. The stage direction said "angry," so he played it angry. The problem with performance notes like the one Akende responded to is that they encourage an actor to play an effect *and actors playing an effect is almost always a cliché.* It's not helpful when writers give an actor performance notes. Not only are you forced to decide in advance what to play, you almost can't help but to decide how to play it. Talk about a recipe for disaster. "He's really sad," "she's really pissed off," "the scene is really intense," . . . and then the actor ends up performing an *idea* of depressed, angry, or intense. The funny thing about playing these clichés is they're not actually what a person would do. Do people always scream when they're angry? Do they tense up when something is intense? Is a depressed person always listless and pouty? But yet that is the way you play it when you decide in advance . . . "oh, he's going to be angry here," I'll yell. My favorite was a sweet young actress whose English was not so great. She was tiptoeing across the stage. I asked her what she was doing, and she replied, "The stage direction said, 'treading lightly.'"

Another result of deciding too quickly how to play something is that you can easily take a fact of the play and jump to the wrong choice. (A choice no doubt based on something you've seen in the movies or on television.) There's a stage direction in the Ayad Akhtar play *Disgraced* for Abe, a young Muslim kid. He's described as "wanting to look very American." To Greg's credit he came in costume to the first rehearsal, but he was wearing a hoodie with a cap. Greg is himself a first-generation immigrant—he's young, a Muslim, dark, fluent in English with no accent, and dresses "like an American" (whatever that means). I've never seen him in either a hoodie or a baseball cap. The fact is: Abe has grown up in a very upper-middle-class environment, having attended private school, and he's very politically aware. Wanting to "look American" forced a knee-jerk reaction with Greg and he went in the direction of "he dresses like a street kid."

There's nothing wrong with saying, "I have no idea what that means." What you can't do is move too quickly and assume you know how to play a fact of the play. It dangerously moves you toward making the text about you and your baggage, rather than what the author had in mind.

JP, if we look at the scene you're working on from the Ara Watson play *A Different Moon*, there was a stage direction where he is supposed to kiss the girl, and even though it was in the middle of a tense, stressed scene, where she'd told you she was pregnant and you felt all your dreams slipping away, you assumed he had a sudden surge of romantic feelings for her. The assumption being, if you kiss someone it must be romantic. It was much more interesting when you played it as a revenge kiss.

We make these mistakes because for some reason we don't believe one of the edicts of the modern theater: the play is not in the words. As soon as you respond to the words as if they are the source of your performance, you're doomed. In the play we're reading in Script Analysis, *The Country Girl* by Clifford Odets, the director, Bernie Dodd, walks into the dressing room, sees the wife of the lead actor, and asks Georgie, "Where's Frank?" If your instant reaction is he's asking for information, you miss the play. In the hands of the right actor, you get the tension in the entire relationship between the director and the wife of the lead actor. This is an important concept to understand. When Bernie sees "the wife" in the lead actor's dressing room, his action is clearly, "What the hell are you doing in here!"

It's important to be aware of the consequences of your choices. Stella encouraged us to number the lines of a script, forcing you to ask yourself: "On what line does the character say something that suggests this decision?" It's so damned easy to go down the wrong road. I should probably do an exercise where we take a fact of the play and see how many wrong decisions you can make. There are an encyclopedic number of possibilities.

Maia pointed how it's very difficult to read the text and not hear a performance going on in your head. The key here is to slow down and specifically address every fact in the given circumstances of the world of the play. Let the facts swim around in your head. Also, don't limit yourself to your first impulse. Chances are it's not just a cliché—it's seldom the most talented choice you'll come up with. Build the play slowly as your belief mechanism takes hold. Stella gave us a great note: "I can believe this much today." It's not possible to believe everything about the character immediately. There are way too many facts. But what you can do is believe a little bit and then add to that. Fight the pressure to come up with a performance right away. When you build slowly and take on only what you can believe, it gives you a road in to a more creative, truthful performance.

Reading a new play is like meeting a new person. Your first opinion is frequently strong and could easily be wrong. Never make assumptions about a play on the first reading. Let it simmer. Sink in. Dig into the text. Live in it awhile. Give it time. The play is not in the words. The words are there to guide you, but they are not the play. The play is underneath, and hidden. It's up to you to uncover it. Don't ever assume you know what a play is about until you have had the opportunity to live with it awhile. Give yourself time to become friends. There is more beneath the surface than you realize.

If you jump too quickly, it'll be a lie. A lie or a cliché. I'm not sure
which is worse.

Why Emails???

One of my many unproven theories is that the responsibility for the end of
great writing falls on the shoulders of the telephone. There was a time when
people wrote letters. Writing a letter took time, it took thought, it took clarity
of what you wanted to say. At the end of this book, I have included a letter
Stella Adler sent to me when I was an actor hopelessly lost in the throes of
rehearsals of a play. It was a very thorough defining of acting. I remember that
when I got it I was overwhelmed by what she'd written. And I've obviously
cherished this letter. I received it in 1980, and I still have it.

Eventually people stopped writing letters, because the phone was so
cheap and immediate . . . so, why go to the trouble? The nature of a phone call
has about it a lack of direction. You can wander all over the place. And when
your plan includes "unlimited" calling, you don't even have to worry about
how long you're taking. When we first started emailing, it seemed as if writing
was going to make a comeback. Emailing, of course, has been replaced with
texting, where almost every element of composition has been dropped. No
grammar. No spelling. No complete sentences or thoughts. A recent article in
the *New York Times* stated that there are only two hundred words used commonly in texts. When I got a text that said, "CU soon," I thought someone
was talking about doing a film and talking about doing a close-up. After my
mother died, I got a text from someone saying, "Sorry for your loss. LOL."
Apparently she thought LOL meant "lots of love." And let's not forget emojis.
I got a text from my friend Ken the other day which said, "Have you seen
all the emojis they've added?" Apparently, we no longer have to even write
a sentence. We can just send a little digital image to express any emotions

or thoughts we might have. I have hopes for emails. I think perhaps we will recover the art of writing.

In 2007, I spent a year teaching in Seoul, Korea. Teaching Korean actors . . . in English . . . through a translator. My assistant and translator, Paul Lim, turned to me during an early class and said, "They don't have that word in Korean." I was horrified. Not only could I not rely on the English language, I couldn't rely on terminology I assumed every actor knew. My vast collection of emails started with Paul. After class, he would send me an email, confirming his understanding of the material covered in class that day. I would then answer his email the following morning. His demand for clarity was extreme. Of course, even in English much of acting is untranslatable, but being forced to clarify concepts in a more practical vocabulary became a turning point in my own teaching.

This collection of emails is a tribute to numerous students who have contemplated class work and rehearsals—and are looking for clarity. When an actor sends a teacher or a director an email with a problem, a confusion, a comment, it's part of the creative exploration of the artist. More than passing you in the hall and moaning about something ("It's so hard!"), taking the time to write something out shows a real concern, borne out of thinking about the issues. The emails I've received over the years and the comments I've included, based on classes or rehearsals, are *from* and *to* some rather extraordinary actors. Actors who think about what they've learned in class or observed and then torture themselves trying to figure out how to use it.

June 3, 2018: As I continue attempting to pull together my collection of emails with actors, there appeared in today's *New York Times* emails between Stephen Spinella and Andrew Garfield. Mr. Spinella won two Tony Awards for playing Prior Walter in the original 1993 *Angels in America* (one for part one and another for part two)—and Mr. Garfield has been nominated for the same part in the current Broadway revival. They've never met, and this has been their first encounter with each other. The emails are wonderful to read. Two actors reflecting on the same role, from totally different time periods— twenty-five years apart.

Stella Adler was a genius. She spent her life trying to find the answer to something that she knew was not answerable: How do you act? She was often quoted, often taken out of context, and often liked or disliked because of her excessive personality. Most often, however, as in the case of my writer friend in Los Angeles who read her collected essays on Ibsen, Strindberg, and Chekhov, she inspired people with her insights.

I spent many years observing at first hand the genius of Stella Adler's approach, and the many nuances of the acting technique and script analysis she taught to actors, directors, and playwrights alike. This book is based on my thirty thousand hours of work with countless dedicated actors, and on my years working closely with Miss Adler. I have taught many, and learned from them all.

Going There—The Place Where Great Acting Lives

What do you think makes for good acting? The performance is believable? It's truthful?—sure, but it isn't enough. You can watch me read a book and it's truthful, but if I'm doing it on stage, you'll want to run screaming out of the theater. Being clear what you're talking about also isn't enough. Understanding the character is great, but it can easily be stuck in a sociology class. Okay, it's many things, but what is the common thread that pulls it out of the mundane? *It's not the words—**it's the experience of the words***.

Teo asked me why I like Meryl Streep so much. My response was: "She's willing to go 'there.'" And then I quickly added, "I'm not sure where 'there' is, but I do know that it's where you have to go if you want great acting."

Dear Teo,

I think one of the reasons I make such a big deal about **connecting** as a concept in acting is because it brings out the human being in our work. For any number of reasons, many of them based on social media, our inability to connect leaves our work sterile. That and the fear of being emotionally exposed. Great actors know they have to expose everything. I once had Miss Streep attached to a film, where the lead character had lost her son in a hit and run accident. Meryl eventually dropped out of the project, explaining, "I'm a mother now and the loss of a child is a place I just can't go." Her performance in *Sophie's Choice* is one of film's greatest performances and it's the story of a woman who had to choose between which of her two children she would let the Nazis kill. But, by the time my film came around, she was a mother and the thought of losing a child was too much. *And she knew where she had to go in order to make it believable.*

Early in her career I coached Kyra Sedgwick for an audition. During our work session, we'd come up with a very strong action: "to pull my husband back from death." We read through the scene, and she sensed I had reservations. "If you really want the part, you've got to go there," I told her. She did it again, and I was stunned at the work. It was scary how open and revealing her reading was. The next day she went to the audition and, when she returned, she told me she felt the audition was merely okay. I asked her why "just okay." "When I walked into the room, the director, producer, and casting director were sitting there and they were such assholes, I didn't want them to see that much of me."

The more you grow as a person, the more you will bring to the table as an actor. But, often, when I watch you work, I see you outside the material. As if you are thinking about it. As if you are trying to decide how someone in that circumstance would respond and then approximating their response.

This ability to "go there" doesn't happen overnight. You also can't force it. But what you can do is start small. You really do expose your veins in acting. It took me forever to let go of years of middle-class "appropriate" behavior. Stella once said to me after a class exercise, "You're a good actor. The thing that's going to keep you from being a great actor is that you're so damned middle class, you think it's unmanly to yell." She meant it metaphorically, but it took me a year to get to the point where my commitment to a monologue was not studied or artificial. I finally made it past being *accurate*. I think that's the kiss of death. I was hitting all the right notes, but it wasn't musical. Or as Stella said to an actor once, "You're hitting the notes, but there's no melody."

It will come in time, but you need to be aware that it's absolutely essential to achieving great acting that you let us see where "there" is. You have to let go . . . and go there.

2
Work Habits

Talk It Out, Don't Write It Out, Don't Think It Out

Give me the part or don't give me the part—I know I'm an actress.

—STELLA ADLER

In college for my final exam in Acting 101, I had to write a journal about a character I was assigned. I got a B+ on "The Journal of Andre Prozorov." We were graded on a curve and unfortunately Jack Heifner (who would one day write the hit play *Vanities*) was in my class and he ruined it for all of us. The result: my final exam performance was very accurate, if not inspired. Years later I was in a production of *Boys in the Band* and I once again had a very thick journal. I even wrote a three-page essay on the meaning of the title. What was missing in my acting work was an ability to translate my notebook into acting. It had not occurred to me that writing uses a different creative muscle than acting. Actors share many similar techniques with writers, but acting is out and writing is internal and private. *Writing down your actor preparation stifles your acting.*

Something happens when you are talking out your work. It allows you to go places that you don't go when you're writing. I'm sure there's a very sound physiological reason for this, but it happens constantly. You talk out your work improvisationally, and the work takes on a life of its own. I was working with JP a couple of days ago on an audition he has tomorrow. Once we moved beyond his need to first memorize it, we talked about the text, the character, other useful elements . . . and, since he had three days to prepare, I left him to do the work. As an afterthought I texted him to say, "Talk everything out." I received a text back from him the next day which began, "I was talking it out and I stumbled on . . ." Same thing happened with Walker. He was standing in line at the bank talking out the past of a character he was working on in class and, aside from the joy of having no one get near him, he made a discovery that made him understand for the first time what it meant to love your choices.

A *60 Minutes* piece on an undercover Federal Bureau of Investigation operative (Tamer Elnoury) preparing for a sting is one of the best examples I could ever imagine of the benefits of talking out your preparation. "It starts the morning that I'm traveling, assume I'm traveling covertly—in alias. I take a shower and put on Tamer's clothes, I put on Tamer's watch, his shoes. I drive Tamer's car. His wallet's in my pocket. His phone is on me. And I drive to the beach and I sit at the beach and I talk to myself out loud like a crazy person, reciting everything there is to know about Tamer Elnoury. His legend, his family. Everything I know about him." He completely defined the actor's process as I see it. With the Federal Bureau of Investigation operative, the stakes are really high. If you get caught, you die. We should no doubt approach every part the same way.

Talking everything out is a key to ownership of the world of your play. Writing out your creative actor work is extremely dangerous. Dangerous because your work ends up on the page, not *in you*. Hearing/seeing the performance in your head is even worse. You try to recreate something you've imagined in your mind.

For me writing was always easier than acting. It made me feel as if I were doing something to get to the life of the character, but I was actually doing the opposite. Some of my notebooks are quite fascinating. But it strikes me that when your actor creative work is on the page, that's where it stays. It doesn't translate easily into acting. That's why novels are so satisfying. The author has done all the work for you. Look at Herman Melville's description of the Spouter-Inn in *Moby-Dick*: "The dilapidated little wooden house itself looked as if it might have been carted here from the ruins of some burnt district, and as the swinging sign had a poverty-stricken sort of creak to it."

He goes on for quite a bit longer, but my point is as brilliant and descriptive as this is, it's on the page. If it were in a play there would at best be a stage direction that says, "In front of him is the Spouter-Inn" or a line of dialogue, "I spent a night at the Spouter-Inn," and the actor would have to fill in the experience of what he's seeing. Writing the novel about it will not help. As a reader it's clear—and its effect is clear—but it's not actable unless an actor turns it into the *experience* of the words.

Many years ago, in a scene study class I had two actors working on the Gentleman Caller scene from *The Glass Menagerie*. At one point I asked the actor playing Jim O'Connor, "What do you think about Laura?" It seemed like an extremely sensible question to ask, but he sort of stared blankly at me. I asked again, thinking perhaps he had not understood what I was asking. Still nothing. "Mark, just tell me. What does Mr. O'Connor think of Laura?" He stared at me desperately, "Do you mind if I look at my notes?"

I'm convinced all this texting is leading to a generation of human beings who are incapable of talking to each other. You can imagine how this is going to impact acting. My brilliant son came downstairs after being in his room for an extended period of time. He told me he'd just broken up with his girlfriend. Through text messages. He had no interest in calling to talk to her about it. I can definitely see the day when the actors text the audience to get them to understand what the play is about.

Talking out is extremely helpful in moving your work off the page—and by off the page, I'm talking about both the text and anything you might write down. In early exercises with Stella Adler, we described something from nature or a photograph from the 1930s. It was the talking it out that made it alive. That's what began to help us enter the world of the play—talking out all your preparation, talking out everything behind the line of dialogue. Building a past. Building the visual images of the place. The props. All of it. And not reporting it, but really entering the world of the play. If I ask you the attitude toward your partner, you will want to do the same thing. Talk out loud your relationship to her. Especially if you start slowly and build as your belief mechanism takes hold. "I can believe this much today." Only take on what you can believe at the moment.

I received an email yesterday from my colleague Sharon Carnicke, who is preparing a lecture on knowledge and belief, and in talking about the premise for her lecture she mentions, "Stanislavsky wrote a lot about the actor's need to believe in the circumstances in the play, . . . and I now think that the more an actor KNOWS about a text, the more belief can be assumed and not stated. So, my topic is Belief from Knowledge." When actors build slowly and take on only what they can believe, they begin to believe it themselves—and, if the actor believes it, the audience will believe it.

If You Must Write, Write Questions

Dear Evan,

I realize you have an uncontrollable obsession with being completely prepared and therefore you like to write everything down, but it's pushing you away from experiencing everything you understand. It's making you slightly distant from your work and from your choices.

I like your idea of *writing interview questions* for your character as a remedy for this. Just make sure you answer the questions out loud. Talk them out. And also don't just approach it as if the answer to the question is the important issue. Give yourself the opportunity to wander around verbally as you talk it out to get to the experience of the answer, a real connection to it. Don't answer questions dryly and allow yourself to answer a question one day and then get back to it the next day and answer it again as if you'd already figured that out. Allow your part to grow. As you think about your character as you walk down the street, let your imagination go where it wants. Just watch out for cars.

Writing questions you have for your character could certainly help your issue of focus and specificity. When you ask yourself a question about your character, your work has begun. "I wonder what she sees in him." "Why would she marry her dead fiancé's brother?" "What does he think about taking four hours to drive home from Yonkers?" "I wonder what it was like to live during the Depression." Any question you ask about the facts of your play is the beginning of your actor work. You might not be able to answer the question right away, but the work has begun. Eventually you need to answer the question as the character, but even knowing what the questions are gets the juices going. Don't forget that part of the acting process is the idea of growth. The more you know about your character and their relationship to the play, the more depth will exist in your answers. Go back to your questions constantly—as you rehearse and keep discovering something new. It doesn't stop at the end of today's rehearsal—or on opening night.

As with everything about acting: "the way you say it is the way you'll do it." It's not just a matter of answering the question out loud, it's answering the question with a connection to what you're talking about. Once you move on to building a past or working though character traits, this talking everything out feeds right away into what is happening. It's certainly true that you know when you're lying. There's something that comes out of your mouth that just doesn't sound right . . . Stella: "When you lie on stage it should hurt" . . . and by that she meant, when you know you're lying. The play is already a lie. You're not Hamlet. You're not in Elsinore, but you want to build those particular lies so they sound like the truth. Talking out the answers to your questions can help you.

Questions and Answers: Documentaries

This email from Abel: I was watching a documentary online and I wondered: How do you interview and ask questions; and how do you figure out what questions to ask? I want to learn how to ask the right . . . or good questions.

Good for you, Abel. It's an excellent frame of reference to approach work on a character. It's as if you're doing a documentary on them. Watching documentaries is good for an actor, because it involves watching human beings respond. Also, you're correct in assuming it gives you a key to what questions you want to ask your character.

The premises of a play and a documentary are the same. There's something you're trying to say with the documentary in the same way there's something the author is trying to say in a play. The actor work is: what is this a play about? It's often difficult to answer the question when it comes to a play, and the same is true for a documentary. The more you work on it, the more insights you have.

The documentary I'm working on at the moment fell into my lap and I did not really have time to research it in depth, which has caused something of a problem. But I had no choice. My student, Walker, found out at the age of thirty-nine that he was a donor baby. Several months later he discovered who his biological father was and reached out to his father's family. He discovered that his biological father was a Broadway publicist who had died of AIDS in the early 1990s. Unbelievably, his biological father's family was coming to New York to visit relatives and Walker had arranged to meet them for lunch . . . in five days! Even though I had no idea what the documentary would be about, the story intrigued me—and I knew I had to film it. I enlisted Chris Petrovski to co-direct with me, because I knew he would approach Walker's "plot" like an actor. And I was right. In private interviews with Walker, he asked exactly the questions an actor would need to know in order to play Walker.

The best answer I can give you is let the facts of your play inform the questions you ask. If you're working on the Clifford Odets' play *The Country Girl*, and you know the play takes place in the world of the theater in the 1950s, then let a logical question like "what was the theater like in New York in the 1950s?" be your jumping-off point. Once you go down that road you will find other questions that logically fall out of the first question you asked. Your next question might be: "What was it like to be a director in the 1950s on Broadway?" In the same way that I don't think you can decide in advance how you're going to perform the character in a play, I don't think you can decide on all the questions in advance. The rehearsal process is a revelatory process. You must let it happen. The questions you ask evolve the same way. They just happen. It's extremely important that you never sit on your impulses. They may take you nowhere, but something will come out of it.

In my friend Deb Margolin's playwriting class at Yale, she has the class do something called automatic writing. Basically, you spend about five minutes writing anything that comes to mind. Just letting your mind free associate. As Deb says, "Even if it's lyrics to a Beatles song, just keep writing."

You want to do a similar thing with your acting. Just keep talking. Not every decision you make is going to be worthwhile, but it will lead you to something else. And that's the important thing. One of the important elements of the road into your talent is the ability to edit your personal debris and find the gems.

Talking While Driving

Preparing for an audition can be a horror. What do you work on? Do you recite lines? Do you act out your part? Do you breathe deeply and do push-ups? Talking out the impulse for the scene you're about to do is a great preparation. In the same way the Federal Bureau of Investigation undercover operative sat on the beach talking out everything he knew about his invented undercover character, an actor has so many possibilities of what to talk out. If you've done all your homework, then owning the impulse for your scene should be helpful.

Dear Akende,

Yes! What a breakthrough!

It was a great question to ask yourself about the character in your audition scene, "What is going on with Freddy when he's driving to the house?" In trying to figure out the answer to the Freddy question, you made several important breakthroughs. First of all, you analyzed the text and figured out what impulse would take you into the scene most effectively, based on what was going on beyond the plot. Second thing, you were shopping for choices. You knew the choices you first made weren't bringing you to life. In fact, they were deadening you. It's an enormous leap when actors stop making any old choice, just to make a choice. Or take the first thing that comes along. It moves you out of being merely a functional actor. You really dug in to find something that fed you. Something you really liked. And you could feel it when the choice was good.

The other thing you made work was you *talked* it out, you didn't *think in your head* how to perform it. You began to talk as if you were him. Talking out what was going on with him. I could tell when you were telling me a day later that you completely owned the experience of what you were talking about. You once again had the experience in you. Even the next day you could use your preparation and be ready for the scene.

Acting is out. There are no cartoon bubbles above your head explaining what is going on. I honestly think there's some sort of feeling in your body when you're in the mode of totally experiencing something. Talking out is one of those things some of us do in life constantly. You have an argument with someone and you're trying to re-write what you said as an "I shoulda said" moment. You completely experience everything that happened during the fight. You see your partner; you see the room. You sort of morph back into the given circumstance of what happened. When you live in New York, you see it on the street constantly. People having complete conversations in some invented world.

It's how I envision the use of improvisation. You're improvising what's going on. And really letting your work go where it wants, free associating without any restrictions. "The sonuvabitch thinks he can do it without me" threw you into the moment. You were there. You owned the way Freddy sees the world. You completely lived off of the world you were in.

This is what we're trying to do with every part we play. Own our character in the character's created world.

3
Mine Fields

I Relate to Him!—And the Russian Word *Razbor*

One night in class, Stella Adler asked a girl why she had chosen to work on the Eugene O'Neill play *Anna Christie*. The girl replied, "Because I related to her." Stella suddenly shrieked, "Why! Because you're a WHORE! And you've slept with every man in town!" Somewhere . . . someone . . . told actors that *relating* to a character was a good thing and required no additional work.

Dear Mel,

You made an innocent actor mistake. You read the script and said, "I relate to him. I've been through a lot of the same things."

The problem with this is you are misled into thinking it's all you need. I know you don't really think "that's enough," but somehow the idea "I relate to this guy" cuts off much of our actor work. If the character were a militant lesbian ex-nun, you would know you have nothing in common with her and you would have done massive amounts of work in order to play the part. You are in dangerous territory, because you do actually have a sense of what your character has been through, but at the same time, if you're not careful you won't dig into what that means. Or *might* mean. Truth is, it's much easier to play a character that is nothing like you, because you have no choice but to start from scratch.

There is an interview with Daniel Day-Lewis in today's *New York Times* (December 26, 2017). "I've explored so many different worlds, but the thing they have in common is they were always entirely mysterious to me in the beginning, probably a great part of the allure—discovering something that seems beyond reach, sometimes impossibly beyond reach, that pulls you forward into its orbit somehow." Mind you if you're playing Abraham Lincoln or the Phantom Thread, you know you don't know anything when you start so, of course, it's going to be mysterious.

I heard Eddie Redmayne at a Q&A for *The Theory of Everything*, and even talking about his process a year later, you could tell how thrilling it was for him. Getting a movement coach, doing research on ALS, meeting with the families of ALS victims, studying pictures of Stephen Hawking . . . all of that wonderful actor process. When a character is nothing like you, you automatically move into your actor process. You absolutely **must** do the same thing with a character "you relate to."

In the play you're doing, you might have known what made you relate to him, but you needed to dig more and figure out exactly what that meant, what effect it had on you, and more specifically you needed to ask, "Does the same thing apply to the character in my play?" The character you were playing was having a lot of mindless sex, which apparently was your case at one point in your youth, but you really needed to dig down to get to what that did to you, what it made you feel. Really connect to that specific part of it and not just the general plot. Maybe, you cut off emotionally . . . or maybe you lashed out . . . or perhaps you sank into oblivion. Maybe it left you empty. Hell, you might have even loved it. So many possibilities. Once you're clear on that, you can leave you and go to him. Figure out, in terms of the play and this character, whether any of your experience might apply to him. The point is, you have to be clear beyond "I could relate to him." And, most importantly, it must be translated into something actable.

It is essential you have a sense of the play you're in and what, if anything, applies to your character in this circumstance. I was struck by the dedication Mart Crowley made to the original cast of *Boys in the Band*, when accepting the Tony Award for the revival of his play: "To the nine brave men who did not listen to their agents when they said their careers would be finished if they did this play. They did it." It was one of the things that was wrong with the recent revival. All the characters in the play are gay, and all the actors on stage in the revival were gay, and no doubt they related on that level. But they completely missed that this play was about a period when gay men were not even close to being liberated. The play even takes place a year before the Stonewall Riots, so living their lives in secret was the norm. And, believe me, no one wanted to be gay, because it was terrible to feel completely rejected by the world you live in. At the end of the play when Harold says to Michael, "You're a homosexual and you don't want to be. But there is nothing you can do to change it," it had no resonance in this latest production, because Jim Parsons is a fabulously adjusted person and is no doubt relieved that he's gay.

Chris Petrovski played a homeless heroin addict, who becomes a militant Muslim, in a film he did last year. Greg, who happens to be Muslim, was in my production of Ayad Akhtar's *Disgraced*, playing a kid who becomes an impassioned Muslim. Chris is not Muslim (or a heroin addict), so every step of the journey was a mystery. Greg, though, was constantly struggling with the difference between his relationship to being Muslim and his character's. My point being, sometimes it's easier when you don't relate to the character.

There's no avoiding what you know, nor should there be, but there is a danger if you assume too much—you will miss the joy of acting. Those rich opportunities borne out of limitless possibilities. That joy that comes from making kick-ass actorly choices that bring you to life.

Relating to a character can give you a road in to the part and the world he's in. But you have to dig deeper to find the play . . . to find what the author is saying. I love the Russian word *razbor*—from an actor's point of view it means digging deep to get down into the depths of the play. Getting to the bottom of what's really going on. I'm fairly certain we need to add that to our acting vocabulary. Starting as if you know nothing is, of course, impossible. But stopping yourself from built-in assumptions means you have the possibility of better choices and opening your actor instrument to creative choices. It forces you to look specifically at all of the facts of the play and really let them resonate. It's the only way you can get to Mr. Day-Lewis' mysteries.

Stop Seeing Text as Sentences

This is what you must rehearse, so you know the sequence of your points. You will automatically move from one point to the next. But if you do this only by words you will have too hard a time to memorize and the memorizing kills the talent.

—Stella Adler

A play is a sequence of thoughts, not a sequence of words or sentences.

I once showed Gustavo Dudamel the opening couple of pages of *Carmina Burana* and asked him what he saw. He said he saw phrases. Not notes!!! Phrases! We should be approaching our work the same way. Seeing a sequence of thoughts. Not sentences! And certainly not words. But then, I suppose that's why he's Gustavo Dudamel.

During rehearsals of an Oliver Hailey play, I asked an actor, "Why are you stopping at the end of every sentence?" To which he replied, "I'm honoring the writer's punctuation." You need to be clear about this. **The punctuation**

is the writer's; you must make your own. I wish actors would stop the habit of seeing text as a series of sentences.

> Dear Michelle,
>
> An important concept in acting is the idea that **a play, a scene, a monologue . . . is a sequence of thoughts**. Not sentences . . . thoughts. And not one thought, but a sequence of thoughts. And, not surprisingly, one thought leads to the next thought . . . which leads to the next . . . which leads to the next . . . and on and on and on.
>
> You're still reading a monologue as if it were a collection of sentences—with periods at the end of each one. As a result, you nosedive at the ends of sentences, and you die out.
>
> I saw a Sony Classics movie the other night, *White Crow*, about the early years of the dancer Rudolf Nureyev. I wouldn't normally quote a movie script, but *White Crow* was written by the British playwright David Hare, so I'll make an exception. In the scene between Nureyev and his teacher, Pushkin, the teacher is explaining dance to him. "The steps have a logic. You need to find that logic, not to force it. One step follows another, with no impression of haste. Or effort. Steps follow. And belong."
>
> If you can deal with the metaphor, acting is exactly like that. There is a logic in the text which you need to find and then let one thought follow the other, without rushing it, so it all fits together.
>
> Stella suggested to us when we begin to work on the text, first read it through—once or twice, and then *do it*. Not recite it as if you were memorizing it, but actually *do it* **in your own words**. You won't get everything. Fine. You might only get one or two things. You get what you get. Look back over it again. If you missed something, add it when you do it again. If you get some of the writer's words, it's fine.

You're not consciously attempting to avoid them, but the important issue here is you are getting a sense of the thoughts. Not the sentences. Stella Adler quote: "Speech without improvisation is death." If you're getting a sense of the thoughts, then you're getting what the play is about. What the writer is trying to say. Doing it this way also makes it easier to find the transitions from one thought to another.

I've actually often thought of doing this with a whole play. Having a read-through of the play and then putting down the script and improvising it. (The only reason I abandoned that fantasy was because I stopped having read-throughs of the script, but that's another story.)

The British call the end of the sentence (the "period") a "full stop," and that's really what actors do when they approach the text as a series of sentences. They memorize a sentence and then dwindle out, both audibly and melodically—leaping into a full stop. The play stops. The energy stops. And then you have to build it up again for the next sentence. It forces you into a perpetual state of recovery. Stella not only suggested we go through a script and take out all the punctuation, she even advised if we have to take a pause, do it in the middle of the sentence, not the end. This was all in service of keeping an aliveness to the text.

You can approach figuring out the sequence of thoughts however it suits you. For a long time I would say to myself, "First I talk about this . . . and then I talk about this . . . and then I talk about this." Then I put it into my own words. Saying it as if I am beginning rehearsal. Like I said, I'm not reciting it to remember it or get it right. I'm simply beginning to layer in my thoughts based on my understanding at the moment. Not a performance, but a slow, building process. Borne out of the evolution of my understanding of the text.

I was once working with Jesse on an audition and as we discussed it, it was clear that there were three thoughts in one sentence. Because he was concerned about the sentences, rather than the thoughts, he ran it all together as one action. Once it was clear that there were three thoughts, it allowed him to free associate, so he was really clear what he was talking about and it came to life.

As a part of your process, you need to have ownership of the sequence of thoughts. Don't wait on the text in order to act. Go through, paraphrasing and talking out every sequence, selecting choices that feed into the central theme. The purpose of this initial exploration is to allow yourself to wander around, wherever the topic may take you. "There is a space between the written page and the actor. The space is diminished by the actor understanding the meaning of the words." This result is an idea.

An email from Chris Petrovski: An acting revelation I had that I forgot to mention last week. Or maybe more so a new approach to working. I've started writing all my dialogue out with no punctuation whatsoever and work from that sheet of paper. So much of the time I feel with acting there is some made-up obligation to the writer and serving the writer. Which kind of means nothing when you think about it, and puts this added pressure on the actor to get the words right. It loosens me up and allows me to focus more on the thoughts rather than phrasing the lines which is the biggest problem with punctuation, we die at the period. Or we think it should be said one way without possibly taking a breath or a thought, in the middle of a sentence. Which often makes for the most interesting and real acting. I don't think actors are aware of how much they are influenced by the punctuation and spend so much of the time trying to break out of it, making the lines sound "real"

> *as opposed to focusing on what they're saying and who they're say-*
> *ing it to. I've begun to believe that I have to look at the page as little as*
> *possible otherwise when I speak I see words rather than my partner.*
> *Hand-written with no punctuation removes the pressure in my mind*
> *of knowing this was written by someone and that I must get it right.*

Not Everyone Can Act

In the same way you have to have a knack for sports, there's a knack for acting. I was told a story in college, which I'm not sure is actually true, but I
always liked it: When Stella Adler and Stanislavsky were working on the elements involved in acting, they had put various concepts in circles on a chart.
Among all the labeled circles, there was a circle with nothing in it. Presumably Stella asked Stanislavsky, "What is that?" and presumably Stanislavsky
said to Stella, "I don't know what that is. But I do know that if you don't have
that, it doesn't matter how much of the rest you have."

How Do I Know I'm Making the Right Choice?

Edith J. R. Isaacs in her introduction to Boleslavsky's *Acting: The First Six
Lessons* has a quote I like: "An actor cannot be made between luncheon and
dinner. He accepts the fact that the profession may take a lifetime of work
and that it is a profession well worth the work of a lifetime."

Due to a sad failing in our educational system, we are driven to find
the right answer rather than embrace the process. Giancarlo brought it up
in class the other night. We don't fall in love with learning when we're in
school. There's no emphasis on process. Only product. So, first, try to get out
of your head the idea that there is a "right choice." Part of the hidden secret
of talent is the ability to "know" when you're on the right track. Something
inside makes it feel right. Also, when you're on the wrong track. It's sort of

like being in a relationship that you know is a mistake. You somehow intuit it's a mistake going into it—or certainly once you've been in it for a while.

Dear Paul,

Stella once said to a frustrated young actor, "Darling you're at step one. You want to be at step eight. You must go from two to seven to get there." It's the great thing about acting. You're always learning and the more you do it, the more you allow yourself permission not to have the answer—and be okay with that. Let yourself off the hook. *Pentimento* in art describes a visible trace of a painting beneath a layer of paint on a canvas. In today's *New York Times* there's an article about the discovery of a Monet water lily painted beneath one of his famous paintings of a wisteria. It's quite common, especially with the advances in today's technology, to discover that underneath the Caravaggio you're enjoying (because you got rich on a television series and bought one), there are a number of instances of changes the painter made before the final painting was finished. Picasso started working on any number of paintings that weren't working, so he painted over them. Even Mr. Picasso went down the wrong road occasionally. Join him. And don't beat yourself up about it.

It's important to think of acting, and particularly rehearsals, as an ever-evolving discovery, rather than an attempt to be right or wrong. You have to give yourself permission to be going down a road that feels right—and then during rehearsals you change your mind. It suddenly doesn't feel right after all. You think you've got it and then you realize you're dead wrong. Definitely this is part of the process. Every time I consider something like this, I realize how frustrating acting is, but also how you have to allow yourself to grow with your understanding of the craft.

More important than worrying about getting it right or wrong, I want you to be alive with possibilities. Creative possibilities. You are a good actor. But you want to be a great actor. And the thing that is keeping you from being a great actor is that you have not reached a level of personal exploration where the result is a revelation. Something unexpected. Yes, you always surprise me . . . but it's because you don't play the cliché, not because you've given me some kind of chills or revelation or insight . . . whatever you want to call it. I think what gets actors work is they come up with something no one has thought of. That's why I keep urging everyone to keep shopping for choices. And not to take the first thing that comes along.

In that wonderful documentary on Marlon Brando, *Listen to Me Marlon*, he brings up something that in my mind made Marlon become "*Marlon!*" He said, "Be surprising. Think of a way no one has ever done it before." There should be an active pursuit of something no one has thought of. It's not just enough to be truthful, you have to add to it an element that lets us in on your talent. A great Brando quote from the documentary: "You want to stop that movement from the popcorn to the mouth. Get people to stop chewing." This is not something you can do without allowing yourself to take the time to let the facts simmer a bit. Embrace the process. Don't clutch. You have no idea when a choice you love will hit you, when there's an element of surprise in your work. "Where the hell did that come from?" It leads to an unexpected performance of a line of dialogue.

4
Essentials

Deadly, Deadly Facts

Facts are death to the actor until they are fed through the imagination and become the experience of the facts.

—Stella Adler

A play has an encyclopedic number of facts. Knowing what they are is essential, but merely knowing what they are isn't enough. And certainly merely reciting them has nothing to do with acting.

> Dear Greg,
>
> Every play has a multitude of facts. An endless number of facts. "It's winter." "It's Paris." "I'm a lawyer." "I lost most of my platoon during the war." "I drove home from Yonkers five miles per hour." As an actor it's vitally important to understand that the facts are absolutely crucial to the life of the play, but they are not meant to be dead pieces of information that you write down as part of some journal you were told to keep. They are specific to the world the writer has created.
>
> Knowing what the facts are and reciting them is not enough. **The fact you say it doesn't make it true.** As an actor, you have to fight the tendency to recite unearned text. In class today, when you said your character was a lawyer, you had no idea remotely what that meant. Even if you had a small, day-one relationship to it, I would have bought it. But you just answered the question as if knowing the information would give you the part.

When I asked you your relationship with Peter's character, you kind of grabbed at straws and said, "We've known each other since we were kids." There was not an iota of truth in the statement, even though you and Peter actually have known each other since you were kids. If you say something like that you at least have to consider what knowing someone your whole life would mean. There was none of that present. You took a stab in the dark answering a question and you came up wanting.

Not only are the facts of a play meant to be alive, they are meant to get you thinking and to get your creative juices going. The writer chose them for a reason, and the actor has a responsibility to fully live them. All of these possibilities are there to feed into your understanding of the play. And, more importantly, every fact of a play is an opportunity for your actor talent to surface. Without experiencing these facts, you simply cannot bring the play to life. Hell, you can't do a television script without bringing them to life.

When Jerry said his coffee shop was in Paris, it had so little life, I would have thought it was Paris, Texas. A coffee shop in Paris! My God! What could be more wonderful! The relationship to the facts, how they fill you, how they bring you to life . . . these are essential. Otherwise the facts are dead on the page and therefore deaden your work.

This is not totally your fault. Actor training has been diminished to a recitation of facts, mostly because of a pressure to get the answer to every question correct. As if the correct answer will give you the ability to act. Time and time again I find that if I ask actors a question, they'll leap to an answer as quickly as they can, as if they were in a class where everyone raised their hands to be chosen first by the teacher. Peter was totally stymied by my constant railing at him,

"You're answering the question too fast." He had no idea what I was talking about. After all, he'd written pages and pages on his character. He certainly knew the answers, but knowing the answers doesn't give you acting. Owning the *experience* of the answer does.

The process to get from the *facts* of the play to the *experience* of the play is what the actor's technique is about. And every time you go back to a fact, you see it more clearly, you understand it more thoroughly, there's more detail. You begin to *believe* it more. You connect to it. The experience of the fact is *in* you.

Working out loud rather than writing your choices down (or merely *thinking* about them) begins to open up the actor's instrument to the *experience* of every choice and every line of text. There's an almost physiological response when the actor is totally connected, when the understanding penetrates not only the mind, but the bones and muscles and skin. For some reason in the Benedetti translation of the works of Stanislavsky, he backed off of the translation of a word Stanislavsky used. In Russian: *dukh*. The spirit/soul. You connect to your choices on a deep level and achieve that joyful moment: "I've got it." And if you believe what you're talking about, the audience will believe it. And it's thrilling.

It's the reason I hate those five damned questions that some acting teachers insist you have to answer in order to play a part. There's nothing wrong with the questions. It's just the belief that answering them is all it takes. My friend, Belita, who coaches acting in Los Angeles, told me the other day that in Hollywood they now have ten questions. It boggles the mind to imagine what they might be!

There is a difference between how an actor answers a question and how a fourth grader answers a question. If an actor tells me their play takes place on the Lower East Side of New York during the

Depression, it should kill me with the difficulty of that truth. Not make me check "c" on my multiple-choice exam. Stella Adler's bumper sticker: **"Facility is fine, but greatness must be paid for in blood."**

If I tell you the biggest sin of an actor is reading a piece of text and deciding how to say it without taking in the facts of the play, I would say the second biggest sin is reporting a fact of the play without paying the price for it. I had the good fortune of meeting Ellen Barkin at dinner recently. We began talking about acting and what I was working on in class—which happened to be the process of experiencing facts. Ellen was a natural. I asked her what went through her mind when I said the play takes place in winter. She said she thought of scarves and a coat and fur hat—and what was fascinating was you felt she was putting them on. Her head went back as she said "scarf," her shoulders sort of hunched up as she said "coat." I think that's what happens when you're experiencing the facts. Every fact brings you to life. Not just emotionally, but physically, spiritually . . . your whole body.

The actor's connection to the part and the character's world is what brings a play to life. And the more gifted the actor, the more in-depth the choices are in making this fiction real.

It's Not an Essay!

Understand and experience all aspects of a choice. Do not trivialize it. Don't romanticize it. Know the nuts and bolts of it. Let your choice bleed into the monologue. Don't aim for simply being accurate, let the spirit of your choice, and your preparation flow into the monologue.

—Stella Adler

I think we keep having to come back to the idea that the play is not about the words. The audience doesn't come to the theater to hear words or sentences.

The belief that we, even for a minute, entertain the idea that our actor work has to do with coming up with a way to say a line of dialogue is completely counterproductive to good acting.

What we're trying to find are the tools best suited to experiencing what is actually important in a play. And that would be: What is the author trying to say? When the curtain comes down, what do you, the actor, want the audience to feel . . . to think . . . to know. What should they be talking about as they walk up the aisles? Is it possible to stimulate them enough so they don't check their cellphones? (Okay. I go too far.)

Every play is about something. A theme. An idea. An enlightened idea. An idea that has existed from the beginning of recorded time. And we as theater artists are given the honor of presenting these vital and important ideas to an audience. Our job is to interpret the play—not just play the part.

The challenge in acting is translating this knowledge to something actable, keeping in mind, "you know more than your character knows." Your characters don't know they're a theme, but unless you, the actor, know this, you will never get depth in your characters. The theme of the play is a jumping-off point for all your actor choices. And it's not an academic understanding of the theme, you really have to know in the depth of your being how big the idea is.

I'm including several emails between Teo and me, as he sorts out for himself the issue of themes and actor choices . . . and also what happens when you come up with something that fights what's in the script:

> Dear Milton,
>
> Ok. This is becoming much, much clearer. So the theme is serving as a compass—if you will—in making choices. I guess I never made that connection. I mean I kinda did, but never really sat down and

thought of it. Maybe that's why I get confused so easily. My problem is I don't make a choice that is connected to the big idea of the play, right?

But there are plenty of ideas in a play or a script. I mean when I read one page of dialogue I feel there's easily three or four ideas in it, am I right? And somehow they all fit in the overall big idea of the play . . . ?

Dear Teo,

It's digging in depth down to the human condition. Really finding the struggle in human terms. This struggle is the jumping-off point for the writer and what the writer is trying to get the audience to understand by experiencing the play. It doesn't mean that it's going to necessarily work out for the character. Each element feeds the theme in a different way. Most actors have a tendency to play a "general" relationship to everything, and their performance is static. Having a clear relationship to everything that happens to you, everything that you talk about, everything you do . . . well, makes sense. That depth adds colors to your performance.

I built this whole past about him being an orphan and then falling in love with the girl and her getting raped and then him going crazy (thinking that it'll give me something that I need but first—I moved too far away from the script, went down the wrong road and second—I don't think that's what the script is about.)

Yes . . . this is exactly an example of going down the wrong road. Keep this in mind, Teo. The text is the basis for every choice you make. If there is no indication in the script that he is an orphan, it doesn't make sense to make that choice. You did the same thing in the scene about telling your brother what an asshole his father was. There was no indication in the script that he had had this conversation "a thousand times." It's a completely different play when that is true. I think what you're doing is feeling the pressure to make a choice—and so you make any choice, just so you've made one.

You're trying to find a connection to a choice, which is absolutely crucial to your actor work, but you can't make any ol' choice, just to connect. Of course, you're going to feel something if she was raped, but merely feeling something is not the point. In fact, you're building a totally different play. If she had been raped, there would be a different outcome for the rest of the play. It's not just about feeling something; it has to feed the play you're in. Any number of choices might feed you, but you must be careful that your choices come out of the play you're in. Be clear what in the text leads you to what you've chosen.

The key to this, if your initial work isn't igniting you, you have to dig more. You have to get more specific. The more detail . . . the more specific, the bigger the payoff. That's the work of being an actor. Some facts of some plays are just more difficult than others. But, damn, that's the adventure.

There's no question this is all hard work. Look at the play we saw yesterday, the Donald Margulies play *Long Lost*. The actors didn't go down the wrong road; they didn't go down any road. There is a huge fact in this play. The brother, while smoking crack in the family house, caught the house on fire and killed their parents. I have no idea if the actors playing the brothers could have written an essay on guilt, but they certainly couldn't act it. I have no idea what they worked on, but they certainly didn't work on the given circumstances of the play. Not one single fact of the script was explored by any of the actors. I don't know when I've seen a play that so violently rejected everything that had been given to them in the text. I'm glad we saw it. It's educational to see what happens when actors play the words and the sentences—and not the world they come out of.

I think what the writer is trying to say is that this can happen to anyone, so it makes more sense to me when I say that he was a normal middle-class guy with a steady income, a good job, brought up by both parents, etc. And I like the choice. I don't doubt it. I can hold on to it.

Everyone has a past, which is unique and different, but there is a clear identity that comes from the kind of play where the middle-class character is involved. It's why great plays avoid the curse of being a "museum piece." The human being in the audience has the same makeup as the human being on stage. We recognize ourselves in these plays.

Earn What You're Talking About

I've never liked the word "earn" when it comes to acting (it sounds too much like it has something to do with a job), but it really does sum up what you have to do when it comes to the facts of the play and the choices you make. It also is an explanation of what's wrong when you don't do it. I would hate to start a list of performances I've seen with "unearned" choices. Add to that the knowledge that you have to pay a bigger price for "my mother is a morphine addict" than you do for "there is cold air coming through the window."

Dear Michelle,

Take your time. Don't feel such an obligation to perform the text. Have a clear idea what you're talking about. You've chosen a quotation about "destiny." What is destiny? What do people think it is? Where do they make mistakes about it? Be clear about the importance of the quote—the size of the idea. Build what's behind the quote slowly, out loud, so you get the accumulated experience. When you finally say the quote, we will get a sense of this huge relationship you have to it. You will have earned it.

In class last night there was a great example of being aware the price you would have to pay for a fact of the play. The character is a German Jew, who fled with his mother from Nazi Germany when he was eight years old. And then in his early twenties he was drafted into the American army where he would invade Germany and eventually liberate a concentration camp. I confessed that if I were playing the part, I would have to work for a month before the first rehearsal. In fact, Chris worked for a month before filming the movie where he played the homeless heroin addict who becomes a militant Muslim. Not only do you have to have a sense of the difficulty of the facts of a play, you have to have a sense of what you have to do to get there.

Don't rush. Really find each thing you're saying. Someday you'll be able to work faster, but for the moment take your time. Take the time to really look at your quote and figure out what it means.

A warning: careful that you don't anticipate what your response is going to be. This is one of those fine lines with acting. You know where you're headed, and you may have some idea how it's going to affect you, but don't play the effect before you start. You can't really think in terms of "This is an important idea, I'm going to play it importantly." It's difficult because there's an actor habit of playing something the way you think it should be played, or how some director told you it should be, or as Akende said, "The stage direction said 'with anger,' so I got angry."

Part of the fundamentals of being an actor is developing the ability to sense the size of what you're talking about, and then figuring out what it takes to earn it. This relationship is essential in making actor choices. When you're talking about people being able to shape their own destiny, you are challenging them to take charge of their lives. That's big stuff.

It's one of the keys to doing big plays. The ones you want to do. Even doing plays by a writer like Neil LaBute without knowing the massive, earth-shattering difficulty of relationships between men and women that he writes about, you'll be in danger of playing it like the television actors who normally do his plays. Actors who think that the script is a collection of funny lines. Yes, they're funny, but they have an important reflection on our times. And if actors don't let people know, they're never going to get it.

I'll Have Tomatoes, Cucumbers, and Some Toilet Paper

No writer writes a list for an actor to report. I should extend that: no writer writes a fact to have it reported. Everything is written for a reason, and everything feeds into what the writer is saying. *You must have a relationship with every word that you speak.*

I would like to think this is a rare problem, but it isn't. The text gives you a series of events or plot points, and actors consistently report the events as if they were reading a grocery list. *All My Sons*: "You remember, overseas, I was in command of a company: . . . Well, I lost them . . . Just about all . . . It takes a little time to toss that off." *The Glass Menagerie*: "I didn't go to the moon. I went much further." *Death of a Salesman*: "Suddenly I realize I'm goin' sixty miles an hour and I don't remember the last five minutes. I'm—I can't seem to—keep my mind to it."

There's a dead tone to reporting—or bringing someone up to date about what's going on. You are not bringing the audience up to date. What you're trying to achieve is an experiential relationship to everything you talk about. The "list" should be alive and vital. And, of course, there's that Valley-Girl melody of speaking these days, where every line lifts up for the last word. It not only makes the list deadly—it bores us to death.

I was overwhelmed with admiration for Ving Rhames in a recent *Mission: Impossible*. He had the unfortunate chore of telling Ilsa about Ethan's (Tom Cruise's) love for his first wife and what had happened. I'm sure on the page it read like the most dull exposition, but Mr. Rhames had so specifically built every event and the past connected to it, it came to life. I stopped eating my popcorn.

Dear Nick,

I understand your concern with having a sameness in your performance of the monologue. And your teacher was right, you need colors and levels, but there is a danger in a note like that. It's easy to artificially solve the problem. ("I know . . . I'll play this loud, I'll play this soft, and then I'll make this cheery.") This is an extremely common problem. It's the reason I started using the term "grocery list." Actors can sound as if they're reporting what they're going to buy at the grocery store. Tomatoes, carrots, cucumbers, and floor wax are all on a list with no specific relationship to anything we talk about. "Siri, put *honey* on my shopping list." There's no relationship to *honey*, it's just an item to pick up at Costco.

It's such a common problem it works its way into Broadway performances. Philip Seymour Hoffman had no relationship to anything he was talking about from the moment he walked onto the stage in *Death of a Salesman*. Willy Loman's first line, while dropping his sample cases onto the ground is "Oh, boy. Oh, boy." Can you imagine what it must be like for a man who's been on the road for forty years to find his cases to be a burden! The line should devastate us, but all it made me think was, "I guess the prop department thought it was okay to have an empty suitcase." Then Philip proceeded to tell Linda about the drive home as if he wanted to bring her up to date. No relationship to: this is the first time he's ever in forty years come back home on the same day he left. No relationship to driving ten miles an hour all the way from Yonkers. No relationship to the four hours he was on the road. He was just giving her facts. A grocery list of events.

As I see it, the solution to this problem of "sameness" is to be clear about your relationship to everything you talk about. And not by superficially adjusting your "performance," but rather a clear experiential relationship to every element of the text.

Writers do not write lists. Even if the line is repeated, it's not because they were afraid the audience didn't hear it the first time. There is a different relationship with every line of dialogue, with everything on the presumed "list." It's very easy in a monologue like this one from Donald Margulies' *Sight Unseen* to make the following sound deadly dull: "I went to pack up his house the other day. My parents' house. All his clothes, my old room, my mother's sewing machine, all those rooms of furniture." It could easily end up as a list of what I did the other day. But, in the hands of a gifted actor, the visual relationship to all the images: "his house," "my parents' house," "all his clothes," "my old room," "my mother's sewing machine," "all those rooms of furniture," can land in a way you see the entire world of his past. It has the potential of being magical.

There's a wonderful documentary on Elaine Stritch, and there's a moment in the documentary where she is in the hospital and she has a monologue to the camera about where she is in her life at the moment. On the page it's three short paragraphs. It's genius watching her, and it's a lesson for actors in the specificity of a relationship to every element of the text. One of my favorite examples in class is showing Meryl Streep's monologue about "the gauntlet" in *River Wild*. It seriously is the worst monologue ever written, but Miss Streep makes it a lesson in acting. Every single thought is specific, and she has a relationship and a past connected to it. She even finds one of the facts of the description so horrifying, she bursts out laughing.

Never "report." I love Anderson Cooper, but he is removed from everything he talks about. If a news anchor talks about two thousand people killed in an earthquake, he might as well be reporting that there's a sale at Kmart. But that's his job. No one wants an emotional newscaster. Walter Cronkite got emotional when he talked about the assassination of Kennedy. It was 1963 and we're still talking about it. If an actor were talking about two thousand deaths it is another matter entirely. On the first anniversary of the September 11 terrorist attack, celebrities came down to the site of the World Trade Center and read the list of everyone who was killed. Until Mark Ruffalo stepped up to the microphone, it was a grocery list of the dead. But when Mark read his list of names, it was heartbreaking. What he had done was the work of an actor. He visualized a person with each name he read.

I'm repeating this point, because I think it's crucial in this discussion. It's what was happening yesterday during rehearsal—you were "playing" how you felt the description should be played. "I should be really emotional here. When I talk about the colors of the painting, I need to really feel it." And so you pushed. It made you tense. Your whole face tensed up. If you push an emotion that isn't really there, you will be lying through your teeth and it quite simply sounds like bad acting. That's the danger of "adjusting a performance," rather than being absolutely, truthfully connected to what you're talking about.

Every line in the play must be justified. You really have to have a sense that the writer put the line there for a reason. They're not just writing dialogue. Not just filling space. If you have a clear relationship to everything you're talking about, variety and color will take care of itself. Take Chris Keller's monologue to Ann in *All My Sons*. There's a specific relationship to everything he talks about: "You remember, overseas, I was in command of a company? Well, I lost them. Just about all. It takes a little time to toss that off."

You must build the specifics of being overseas, of losing almost an entire company of men you commanded. And then another thought:

> Because they weren't just men. For instance, one time it'd been raining several days and this kid came to me, and gave me his last pair of dry socks. Put them in my pocket. That's only a little thing . . . but . . . that's the kind of guys I had. They didn't die; they killed themselves for each other.

You're not reporting a plot about what one of the men did—there is an absolutely specific past and a specific relationship to what his soldier did. Although the action of both of these chunks belong together, the specific relationship to each is not the same. And it's certainly not a grocery list of what happened.

Work slower. Talk out everything one step at a time. Don't go to the final performance when you start. Build a little bit. Build what you can believe and add to it. If you sense it all sounds the same, think about why. If there are no levels, think why. Chances are you're not connecting specifically to what you're talking about. Or you're connecting to everything the same way. There's a difference between tomatoes and cucumbers.

Too Much, Too Little

I had a student report to me the other day an experience in a casting director's workshop. And, by the way, I think casting directors giving workshops
should be against the law. The casting director told him to just, "Do it again
and throw it away. Just talk." Dangerous note, not just because no character
on a major television series is either throwing it away or merely talking, but
giving a **performance note**, especially one that makes it seem as if acting is
just chatting, forces an actor to an unusable place.

To the class,

Acting is like Pandora's box. You let one thing out of the box and
a hundred other things fly out with it. Experiencing the sensation of
being connected is something you are going to need to do for the
rest of your life as an actor, no matter whether you're making choices
for *Hamlet*, *Brighton Beach Memoirs*, or *Madam Secretary*. You must
have a "that's it!" moment, "I got it." It completely frees you up to let
go, because you're clear why you've made the choice you have.

The Pandora's box comes from the unfortunate reality that it's not
just being connected that makes for good acting, it's *how* you're connected. I hate to say this, but today, we had three examples of what
not to do. Akende, Tony, and JP had clearly thought out the direction
they were going before they started. None of them would dare wing
it, but in their exuberance, all three of them fell into some common
actor traps.

Akende was working so hard to connect that everything was
pushed. Emotions were pushed and physicality was pushed, and
vocally it was extremely strained. On the complete reverse end of the
spectrum, Tony wanted to make sure he was being truthful and so he
was so conversational and low key that we got absolutely nothing. JP,

on the other hand, got so caught up in the truth of what he hated, he became uncontrollable. It was scary. I thought he was going to have a heart attack.

Akende's problem was borne out of a very smart understanding of the size of the idea of what he loved. "I love the birth of a child." He knew very well the size of the idea of the birth of a child, absolutely clear that there could be nothing bigger or elevated than the beginning of life. But the muscular tension in order to get there made it feel like "ACTING." The truth of what he was saying wasn't in him as much as he wanted it to be, so he pushed for an effect.

This is something that goes back to the original sin of the actor. Deciding in advance how to play something and then rushing to a performance of the line. Akende decided that such a line of dialogue needed to be played big. So what we got was this big performance, but we weren't sure what he was talking about. It was an actor who "really meant it." This happens so often in all media, it's almost an epidemic. I'm thinking Leonardo DiCaprio in *Revenant*. You're so aware of the actor's performance, you have no idea what he's talking about. It falls in the category "earnest acting," the school of "I really, really mean it. Can't you see how much I really mean it!" or "I'm suffering. Can't you see how I'm suffering."

Tony, who in life has more energy than almost anyone I've ever met, went the other direction. Fearing that he might be too big, he decided to play everything in an overly conversational "see-how-real-I-am" tone. Everything was lifeless, so we had no interest at all in what he was talking about. Everything he said deadened him. When he said, "I walked out the door and ran down the street to catch the bus," it could not have been less interesting. And, bless his heart, he kept saying, "but I can see it." He could see it, but it wasn't giving him anything that was breathing life into the text. And because it wasn't feeding him, it was lifeless.

I'm talking about two different issues here, but they are very intertwined. The first, of course, is deciding in advance how you're going to perform something. Or, in Tony's case, how you're *not* going to perform something. The second is that you want the performance to come out of a relationship to the text. But there's a real clear difference between your intellectual relationship to the text and your experiential relationship to the text. And you cannot force any of it. And in the case of Tony, merely seeing something and reporting something, while it might be truthful, it does not mean that it will translate into good theater.

JP's exercise exposed one of the many dangers of using your own life. While it's fantastic to experience what it's like to connect fully and to uncontrollably get the feeling that happens when you are completely immersed in your choice, what happened with JP was something of an uncontrollable explosion.

The line you chose for the exercise was "I hate my job." Because you do hate your job, the build was honest and truthful . . . but yet uncontrollable. Added to all of the impossible things about acting, controlling the uncontrollable is huge. And it is the biggest problem about going to your own life. In your case, it was an opportunity to explode about something you had perhaps not verbalized before. Or certainly not verbalized so emotionally. Michelle has to fight that tendency as well. She can become so emotionally involved in some of her choices that she starts crying and can't stop.

Rampant emotion on stage not only doesn't serve the play—it's slightly embarrassing. I have no idea why the audience likes it. Maybe they enjoy watching people suffer.

I had a student at New York University who was doing an exercise, which involved waking up in a hotel room. Rather than "miming" a blanket, he brought one to class, which I applauded, but then when he got to the exercise, he endlessly writhed and stretched and I thought he was never going to get out of the bed. I asked him why he went on for so long and he said, "It felt good." His work was often like that and he was really charismatic as an actor, but this indulging his emotions really was annoying. I spoke to my shrink, Babette, about it and she suggested he was working on himself and not the part. I thought that was brilliant and I think that it perfectly defines the essence of indulgent acting. It's actors working on themselves and not the part. You see it all the time. It's very discomforting. It makes the play about you and not what the playwright was after. *Really feeling it* is a dangerous criteria for evaluating your work.

This is the Pandora's box I was talking about. You think you're doing a simple exercise about something you love or something you hate, but you've entered a world where we have to get a sense of "what is good theater?" It's where acting gets very complicated and individual. Akende felt connected, but it was pushed. As loud and explosive as JP was, he certainly was connected to what he was talking about, but it was completely out of control and therefore made the audience uncomfortable. Tony felt something—it was real—but because it was so conversational and thrown-away, it just wasn't good theater.

I attended a concert some time ago of the Grace Choral Society in New York and their performance of Beethoven's *Missa Solemnis*. It was a truly overwhelming performance, and I was struck by this truth about music: the composer has made it clear how he wants certain notes and phrases interpreted. The job of the conductor, the choir, the orchestra, and the soloists is to earn these interpretations.

The performance was moving because of the ensemble's connection to the dynamics, as opposed to numerous other choral groups I've heard where I felt there was an accurate representation of the music, but there was no life to it. I was reminded of the responsibility that comes with being an actor. Not only are we John Maclay (the conductor), we are the singers, the orchestra, and we are also the composer. An actor is the one in charge of letting the writer know exactly how the text needs to be played.

See It, Then Say It

When you say something that is visual, you must make them (the audience, your partner) see it because you have already seen it. Talk to their eyes. Give it away. Don't draw back. Part of being an actor means you give it away. In life we don't give it away. Our habit is to pull it back and check it instead of plunging ahead. It's as if you are perpetually in rehearsal.

—Stella Adler

The ability to visualize is a tool you cannot exercise enough.

The concept is not foreign to us. In life we visualize all the time. If you tell someone about your horrifying Christmas dinner, you see the table, the family, you see the event as it happened. Images abound. In fact, there are almost no moments when we do not access visual images. A brilliant daily exercise for actors is to describe something to someone. Anything. A person you saw, an event you watched, the vegetable display at Trader Joe's. The more complicated and complete, the better. And the more it brings you to life and stimulates you, the more useful it is to your acting.

Another one of my unproven theories is that the emergence of video has harmed acting. If there's an image on the computer screen, why should I bother describing it to you? There was a time when you were buying a new outfit that you would describe it to someone and both you and the person on the other end of the phone would be thrilled and excited. Now you take a picture with your cellphone, and it's a done deal. Describing something to someone for a desired effect is an excellent way to think of visualization. It's not for accuracy, but rather describing to bring something to life, to make an audience have the same emotional connection to something that you do.

Exercises where you describe something from nature or the person you saw at Costco or a whimsical photograph by John Margolies will always help you. In fact, one of the exercises we did in Stella Adler's class was to take a period photograph and describe the scene to the class. I've directed so many plays that took place during the Depression, I can completely visualize the streets of the Lower East Side of New York in the 1930s—as if I'd lived there. The important concept here is that your description brings you to life, you are not just reporting what you are seeing. Also, a key to visualization is to see it first and then tell us what you see. Don't tell us, hoping it will appear.

Dear Greg,

There's a very strong reason we need to address your visualization work. You are simply not digging deep enough to find what excites you about your images.

As actors, we respond to visual images easier than any of our other senses. True—smell is big, but not so easy in acting. While it's true you know what you *do* when you smell garlic in the air of the streets of Little Italy or the smell of kimchi when you get off the plane in Seoul, you can't actually smell it when you're sitting on stage. I know a couple of actors who swear they can do it, but I don't buy it.

It's also true you can hear sounds in your head, but you have to stop the play and concentrate on the sound. Or the music. If I put my mind to it, I can hear Barbra Streisand sing "People," but I have to really focus on it. And I probably also have to have a quiet room, not exactly the optimal condition for acting.

When you consider how much of acting is based on images and ideas, the ability to visualize is one of the most important abilities for an actor to develop. And it's not just that you can see it—it must affect you. It must give you something that feeds your acting. You must live off of it. Maybe it's the color. Maybe it's the delicacy. Maybe it's the strength. Shop . . . shop . . . shop until you find what ignites you and brings you to life.

This is a life note for your acting: You want all of your actor choices to bring you to life. And a great road in to accomplishing this is to be specific. *The more specific, the bigger the payoff.* "It's a beautiful sky" is fine, but you're losing the joy of actor work. The more you dig, the more alive it makes you. The specificity in describing the puffy white cloud, the ribbon of fire-laced sunlight piercing through it, the rich dark blue background . . . is all more alive.

At the moment your visualization work is still reporting what you're seeing with a tinge of pushing how you think you should feel about it. Keep in mind: you need a genuine emotional connection to what you're describing, not one that is forced. Mean it. Have a relationship to it. Depending on the play, you will make choices that help you. It's the joy of acting. We cheat. We know what the play is about so having clear images that feed the play means you don't have to work so hard. The images give it to you.

For the purposes of this exercise, I want you to actually, physically see what you're describing and see it in detail. Not from your memory, not from the television, not from the internet . . . but the actual "something" you're describing from nature. You can research a hurricane later and describe it, but for now I want you to take the actual object and see it, then describe it to us.

Continue to make demands on yourself to dig deeper and deeper with this image work. Visualizing as an actor is key. Create the images specifically. Go back to the images so you can begin to see them with more specificity. Note the difference between "a deep blood red" and "faded old t-shirt red" and the way each image feeds you.

Enjoy going back to exercises. Enjoy the description of the leaf, the wedding dress, the old manuscript, the photo album that the child destroyed. Let your relationship to each of these grow. Find something new. Leave yourself open to the surprise of what you find.

What a Great Wall!

Dear James,

I found your imaginary trip to the Great Wall of China thrilling and I'm copying the class with this email, because so many got bogged down in details that were not helping. You were meant to make us believe that you took a vacation, which you had not actually ever taken. In its simplest form, every play is very much like building an imaginary vacation. Sure, the vacation might be to New London, Connecticut, where you're building the world of *Long Day's Journey into Night*, but you're still trying to make this world believable—and make us believe you're living in it.

James was not only connected to what he was talking about, we all saw and experienced the world he created. In fact, it was so horrifying that only an idiot would ever decide to go there. From the eight-hour bus ride to get to the Wall and then the vendors hawking their mini-Great-Walls at the base of the steps, every single choice he made fed him. Every image was specific and brought the trip to life. This was a perfect example of shopping for choices. He even admitted when he started the research, he planned to like the idea of going, but the more he read the more turned off he was by all of the negative things people had to say.

Keep in mind: the difference between a technique exercise and working on a specific play is that a technique exercise is to develop the tools of the trade, while a play has given circumstances that will dictate your choices. What's important about technique exercises is that they allow you to free associate improvisationally as James did, because you have no limitations. It serves you big time when you get to a play. James invented his own play and then earned it.

When Theresa built her summer working in the Irish pub, which she also hated, it made me think that none of my students like vacations. What was funny about that was Joel somehow missed the assignment and Theresa was so believable he commented, "You're the only person I know who hated being in Ireland." Ah . . . what a success.

Every play is a lie. You are not Hamlet, you do not live in Denmark, your uncle didn't kill your father and marry your mother. And yet this is what you must make the audience believe. (And do it in iambic pentameter!) Stella quote: "Every play is a fiction. It is your job to defictionalize the fiction." She also added, importantly, "You're going to use other fictions to do this; be very careful how many you use. You have to make each one believable."

Building an imaginary vacation is a good start to having a sense of building the fictional world of a play. Everything about a play is filled with images, experiences of the past, relationships to everything we describe, and making someone believe you were in Paris last weekend advances you one step closer to making an audience believe you're a woman named Nora, who's married to man named Torvald and you live in a small town in Norway.

There's a Place for Us—You Must Be Someplace

You are not uncomfortable as long as you know what you are doing. If you know perfectly what you are doing, one thing after another, you can add any dialogue. Become familiar with the room. Say, "I am going to do a definite number of things." Be able to do these things truthfully and with the ease of second nature. Make the room yours. Open the window, the door, move around the room.

—STELLA ADLER

An essential part of building the world of the play is actively being able to both live in the place (the circumstances) and live off of it. It's an extension of our visual work, because so much of what you're living off of is in the imagination . . . because it's not actually there. Obviously, I'm a big believer in talking out everything. I can't say enough how valuable it is to stand in a room and talk out both what is there and what is not there, in an experiential manner. Having a clear relationship to everything around you will absolutely give you grounding in the play.

Every play takes place someplace. Words without a place is an unnatural condition of nature. Words don't take place in a vacuum. If you tell me about a conversation you had with your mother, you see where you were when it happened.

Build the place, out loud. Develop the ability to see what's not there.

Dear Theresa,

In terms of what we're doing in class, *living in the place,* I thought this might help. Chris Petrovski recently filmed an episode of *The*

Blacklist, where he played a hacker. Television moves so damned fast, and as a guest star they were really only interested in giving him one take, so when they got to the scene in "The Hacker's Lair," he asked to be allowed to stay on the set while they were lighting (instead of bringing in the "B" team). Although he only had ten minutes, he made very clear choices about his relationship to everything in the shot. At the end of the take, the director looked at him: "That was incredible. I'm taking you to Los Angeles and using you in my next project." Clearly that was never going to happen, but *building the place* is an exercise that is apparently seldom done by most actors.

It makes perfect sense. In life, think how insecure you are the first time you go someplace. And how confident you become, once you know where you are. The script will give you guidelines as to where you are and your relationship to the place. Even if it's your first time in a place, your relationship will be different than if you come there regularly. And you will build it with that in mind.

Stella said that Brando would go to the set every day an hour before anyone else. He spent time in the place, because he knew his relationship with "the place" would give him an ownership of the part. Chris Carmack related to me his experience on his first day on set of the television series *Nashville*. He said he was petrified but took a moment to talk out a relationship with three items on the set. I even think one of them was the doorknob. But building the place and his relationship to it grounded him. It clearly served him well. He's now a regular on *Grey's Anatomy*. I cannot even imagine the clarity you must have to perform a lobotomy.

Most of the circumstances on stage and on set are completely reliant on our imagination. Our ability to visualize something that is not there saves us. On stage almost everything is imagined. Or maybe it is because of the small theaters and rehearsal rooms I've been in, we are forced into imagining everything. The fourth wall alone is a monumental challenge. And the fourth wall of a film is even worse, a crew of people busily doing their jobs.

Waking up in the dressing room will be the eventual exercise . . . but let's see what happens if we go step by step through it. **Visualize and talk out** the dressing room first. See it in a sequence. Don't jump all over the place. Then, once you have it, put your props in and talk out your relationship to them. Ethan built a dressing room in my Yale class fifteen years ago and I will never forget the dead rose in the vase next to the cracked mirror he described.

The fact that you can visualize the circumstances of your play means that you are not stuck in a vacuum. One thing at a time makes it your environment. One object created fully and truthfully that has a real meaning for you can bring the environment to life.

Do not make choices that deaden you. Don't add a lot of plot that deadens you or makes it sound as if you're reporting some facts. Everything must bring you to life. And if your circumstances bring you to life, then you don't have to work so hard. The confidence you have as an actress, when you know where you are, will shine through.

Make It Yours, Not the Prop Department's

The set designer has given you the radiator. You give it the dripping rusty water coming out of it. The actor's job is to bring the set to life. The set designer may give you the mirror, but the actor's job is to bring the prop to life, and the joy of being able to visually add a crack in the set designer's mirror is that you control what feeds you in the play. Think how differently you will respond to a pristine mirror. Obviously, it depends on the play, but it tells you everything you need to know about the world of this particular actor, when the dressing room has a dead rose and a cracked mirror.

The prop has a theme. Part of building a relationship with a prop: Adding the element of the theme.

Props are as much a part of the physical circumstances of the play as the set is. Your relationship to every prop can "prop you up," if you have a specific connection to it. It's ridiculous to have the prop department hand you a prop—and then you use it without considering how it might feed you. It's all part of ownership of the space you're in, rather than wandering around in someone else's set, using someone else's stuff.

Dear JP,

Good work. The exercise: take an object and build three different connections to it, three different ways to live off of it, was masterful. I love what you did. You chose to build from the point of view of the "idea" of the object.

Let's look at your object: the baseball from your first home run.

You hit on great stuff that was all a part of thinking through the nature of what your object represented. What is the nature of a baseball game? What is the nature of the first time you do something? What is the nature of memory?

Your first choice was a very touching choice. A moment in life you hold on to. Just taking the time to let all of those memories come back to life was like a visitation to another world. Just beautiful.

In your second choice, we got a sense of your inner rage at the idea of how American capitalism had taken over everything you love. Great theme. Something like baseball, meant to be enjoyed as a sport, has become a billion-dollar enterprise.

And your third choice was wrenching: Lost dreams. Dreams unrealized. Stolen dreams. What was particularly insightful were your revelations about the nature of dreams. You even hit on the difference between dreams, fantasies, and hopes.

The discussion made your choices have much more depth. It's this nonspecific work that so curiously leads us to choices in acting. Allowing ourselves to free associate more before we move into the specific actions of a performance.

If we can begin to see these universal themes, these enormous ideas—these ideas that have been a part of civilization since the beginning of time, our work can have an importance. An audience will recognize the humanness of a character.

What you hit on Monday was the ability to connect to your prop and your attitude toward your prop by understanding the theme. It added immeasurably to the past you had built. Not only were you able to live off the prop from the point of view of the theme, it gave the story. Yes, you had a plot—something from your childhood—but more importantly you could see the prop as the idea of a play. And the ability to live off of the prop from this point of view is huge. You're working toward "letting it happen" rather than "making it happen."

> Stella in class: "Do you know what you did wrong? You knew how you were going to behave instead of taking it from the object. Taking it from the situation. The acting is not something that you just do no matter, it's something that gets born."

When you isolate an element as an artist, every time you come back to it, it grows. It's now yours by having isolated it—by selecting it, by having a clarity about it. The more specific you are about this preparation, the more spontaneous you are.

So Stella Adler Says to Marlon Brando

I once asked Stella what she'd taught Brando. He'd just been on *Larry King Live* and had said she'd taught him everything he knew. Stella modestly said, "I never taught Marlon anything. Well . . . there was one thing. He was doing an exercise in class on one occasion and I stopped him, 'Never lie!' He stopped and thought about it, redid the exercise, and he never lied again." I've always loved the idea that Stella caught Marlon Brando indicating. When you lie on stage, it should hurt.

5
Themes

Two Plus Two Equals Four-ish

We are killers in life and we run everything down. We need to get a real sense that plays are about something that is important.

—STELLA ADLER

A play is about something. It is about an idea. A universal idea. One of the biggest struggles we have as actors is both figuring out what the theme of the play is, and then understanding the idea is a big idea and lifting ourselves up to the size of the idea.

We have lost the sense of the size of these ideas. And, as a result, the big plays seem trivial—and worse, actors approach text without any sense of the importance of what they're talking about.

Dear Greg,

Keep in mind: Writers have something they want to say. As an actor, knowing the idea behind a play—and by that I mean the universal idea, the cosmic idea—affects everything. When you're making choices, they become choices that feed the theme and are not choices just for the sake of making a choice.

With the big writers the ideas are big. At a lecture I attended years ago, Arthur Miller described the difference between big writers and little ones. "What big writers have in common is a fierce moral sensibility which is unquenchable and they are all burning with some anger at the way the world is. The little writers on the other hand have made peace with it. The bigger ones can't make peace." The ideas he's talking about are the ideas that have shaped civilization. And it's important we bring ourselves up to the size of this idea. You have to begin to understand the difference between "you gotta light?" and "I'm going to talk to you about something that is important to your life." Speak to the center of people. Reach your partner. Size is not about volume. Stella once admonished an actress working on Nora from Ibsen's *A Doll's House*, "You're playing one of the biggest themes in human history—personal freedom—as if you were talking about a sale at Bloomingdale's."

In a sense, what we have to do is re-educate ourselves in the way we look at the world. There's a difference between how an actor sees the world and how the audience sees the world. The non-artist sees the world as just something that's there to occupy space. As an actor you must begin to see common everyday occurrences as ideas. A father and son playing catch in the park becomes the idea that a father passes on a tradition to his son. I saw a woman on the subway reading to her son. It was beautiful. The noise of the subway against the image of a woman holding her son in her lap, while reading and showing him the words and the pictures. It's the idea of the love between a mother and her child. The rest of the people on the subway were busy listening to iPhones or texting. The mother and child went completely unnoticed. A couple holding hands walking down the street—the need people have for one another. A universal idea. A teacher standing in front of a room full of students—passing on knowledge.

A great exercise is to take a common household item and lift it to the size of a big idea. A pencil becomes the instrument that allows us to look back on all of recorded history. A fork becomes the beginning of civilized behavior. A book becomes our connection to other worlds, other information. A student once broke my heart at New York University. She brought in a small bottle of pills. "These tiny little pills seem very innocent, but they were given to me when I was very young. They are now the only way I can get through a day. They are my lifeline."

Jonathan complained he'd gone out to people-watch on a subway and everyone was on their cellphones. Sad, of course. But this, too, is a big idea. The idea that we are losing human communication.

These are all ideas, but more importantly it's a way we must incorporate into our thinking if we are ever going to do big plays. We see themes and universal ideas on the street constantly. But because we are not seeing the world like actors, we do not really see them in any enlightened sense. We're like an audience who sits back and says, "Show me." An actor should stop being like an audience. We need to all begin to watch the human situation and realize this is the stuff of plays. This is the stuff of the modern theater. As my colleague Deb Margolin points out, "Theater exists because of the failure of language."

Stella once challenged us about how we listen in class:

> Listen to me very carefully, and try and listen not with your ears, because our ears are going to hear words. Listen the way an actor listens. He listens with his blood and when his blood is involved in listening, he hears . . . otherwise he only thinks he hears. We have lost the habit of listening like actors. Listen! Listen! With your ears, with your eyes, with your blood. Nobody listens on the stage anymore at all. It's as if it weren't there.

Listening . . . seeing . . . watching . . . these are all areas where we need to lift our thinking.

Although this has been going on for a long time, it seems to me the inability to understand big ideas is worse today because there is very little sense of how big—and by "big" I mean it's universal, epic importance—certain ideas are. "Friendship" comes to mind. People actually believe they have fourteen hundred friends because that's what it says on Facebook.

I had lunch with Mark Ruffalo several years ago when he was appearing on Broadway in a revival of a Clifford Odets play, *Awake and Sing*. In fact, he had been nominated for a Tony Award for his performance. I had seen the play and was extremely moved, not just by Mark's performance, but by the depths he'd reached in his work on the character. I asked him his "secret." He said that he discovered the through-line action of his character was "to find a home."

Among the many things I realized about that choice was Mark understood the size of the idea of *home*. He wasn't talking about finding a good deal on a rental out of the *New York Times*. He was talking about the human need that one has to connect to a place or the people who complete you as a person.

He had to do an enormous amount of work to find that choice. His dressing room was littered with books on Odets and books on the Depression (the play takes place in the early 1930s); there were pictures of the streets of New York from the period. But once he had cobbled together all of this information, he was able to find this lost soul in the Depression in America where hundreds of thousands of people slept in cardboard boxes and under bridges, and he understood the character's need to find a home.

As I was leaving the Wednesday matinee I attended, the conversation in the lobby was consistent. "My God. This could have taken place today." That is the success of a play. The theme and the humanness of the characters resonate today. I was extremely impressed the audience was getting what the play was about, and not just talking about Mark's performance.

The violinist Hilary Hahn was being interviewed on NPR a couple of years ago. She said that the high point of her career was when her mother told her she was so riveted by her playing, she forgot that Hilary was her daughter. I always think, if the audience comes out and comments on the actor rather than the play, we've failed.

Stella Adler: "There are actors who can say, 'two plus two equals four,' and make it sound like the most deadly piece of dull math in history. And there are those who can say, *'two plus two equals four,'* and make you know that because this is true, we can put a man on the moon."

Theme, Theme, Where Is My Theme? — Size Matters

You are now articulate. That is one of the most important aspects of acting— to be articulate about ideas. The actor must have confidence in himself that he can work on plays that have ideas in them.

—STELLA ADLER

When I was in the eighth grade, Mrs. Moore had us write papers on various short stories. Among the questions we had to answer: What is the theme? How do the characters fit into the theme? I thought it was difficult in the eighth grade, and it hasn't become any easier. But I know once you understand what your theme is, and more importantly the size of that theme, the play takes on a new importance.

This morning I received the following email from a former student:

An email from Alex: "I met a guy on a film shoot from an Eastern European country. Vitali is his name, a director and producer but *was working as an actor in this movie. Another actor asked him what the script is about and he said, 'it's about dreams and following your passions' and I whispered to him, 'you know how I can tell you are trained? You answered with the theme, not the plot.' And he said, 'shhhh, I don't want people to know I am good at what I do.'"*

Dear Walker,

I understand your problem. Finding the theme is not necessarily easy. When the director/choreographer Jerome Robbins was working with the songwriters of the musical *Fiddler on the Roof*, Sheldon Harnick and Jerry Bock, he kept asking them, "What is it about?" They kept coming up with things like, "It's the story of a farmer in Russia," and Robbins would yell, "No! That's not what it's about!" And they'd go back to the drawing board and come back the next day and say something like, "It's the story of three sisters and their Jewish father," and he would once again say, "No! Not what it's about!" Finally they came to him and said, "It's about tradition." And he said, "Yes! That's what it's about. Now go write a musical about tradition." Not only did the show become the longest running musical on Broadway, it has been performed successfully all over the world. An audience understands the idea of tradition and sees themselves in the conflicts that arise out of it.

Themes . . . universal ideas . . . are ideas that have been a part of humanity since the beginning of recorded time. Ideas that affect people, that define them. You leave these plays . . . not with an answer, but a more thorough understanding of the problems of life.

Knowing what your play is about is such relief. It keeps you from wandering around aimlessly, hoping you will bump into a character or an action. You're not just making "any" choice to feed your play. You're making specific choices to feed *this* play. It's the reason *Fiddler on the Roof* was a hit in China. It is a country with an enormous history of traditions. And "tradition" is one of those universal ideas.

When you understand the theme, you have a foundation for all of your actor choices. And when you have a sense of the size of the theme, it will keep you from trivializing what the writer is trying to say. I'm not saying that the plot isn't important. I'm saying it's not what the play is about.

As an actor, you should start by knowing the author has *something to say*—an idea to get across to the audience. And there are characters who struggle through the invented world of the play, making the author's ideas come to life. The author gives us characters who do or do not cope with this created world—and we watch this happen. This understanding gives depth to your work. It gives depth to your work as long as you are able to elevate your thinking to the size of the idea.

Think of it as the *enormous* size of the idea. If I decide that *Golden Boy* is about the personal struggle of a man for his soul, then I have to realize how big that is. Acting is not about answering the question correctly. In my bones, I must understand what "the struggle of a man for his soul" means.

I once heard Arthur Miller lecture to a group of young writers. "You might not be clear what your theme is when you start . . . but once you figure it out, write it down on a strip of paper, tape it to your typewriter, and make sure that everything you write feeds into this idea." The process is similar for the actor. You are not going to read the play and know right away, "This is the theme." Through the rehearsal process, you begin to have a clearer idea what the writer is saying, and this knowledge gives you the confidence to make choices which feed into the author's intent.

I encourage you to continue to take this step where you are not only cognizant of the theme, but you grasp its size, its momentousness. It makes the choices you make to feed into the theme more significant.

Don't Pull the Theme Down to You

There's a famous story about an actor who said to Stella Adler, "Hamlet's confused. I understand that, because I'm also confused. Hamlet's a guy like me." Stella's response was immediate and piercing. "Darling. Hamlet owns Denmark. You don't have a pot to piss in." The actor syndrome of "I can relate to him" rears its ugly head throughout actor work. Nowhere more than in trying to get a sense of the idea of a play.

Dear Cameron,

Golden Boy is not just about a dude who's trying to decide if he should make a lot of money boxing or be penniless playing the violin. It's about an entire world that exists which seduces you into destroying your soul. Buying you for a price. Joe wants those cars that whiz by him in the park and he wants the world those cars represent, but he also wants the happiness that comes from simply sitting and playing his violin. "With music I'm never alone when I'm alone—Playing music . . . that's like saying, 'I am man. I belong here. How do you do, World . . . '"

The issue here is what your relationship is to what the play is about. You have to lift yourself up to the size of the idea of the play. It shocks me that your director suggested that, in the scene with Lorna, you think about your relationship with some girl at drama school. Especially when you're working on a play as huge as *Golden Boy*. Quite honestly, of all the stupid ideas of acting I have ever heard, that one is in the top three. It completely eliminates the fact that a playwright has something profound to say. Unless your girl from drama school is a hooker from New Jersey, who's having an affair with a manager who wants you to sell out your soul—then your acting partner is really useless to you . . . at least as a useful image for this play. If you spend time pulling everything down to you, not only will plays suffer, you will never grow as either an actor or a person.

It's not that you *play* a theme. Your character does not know he's a theme. You know more than your character knows. He just lives his life. But once you are aware of the idea of the play and the elevated importance of the idea, it informs your choices. It puts you, the actor, in a kind of mindset that keeps you from trivializing the text. You are God speaking ideas that are important to humanity. Maybe that's how we should approach acting a play. Like parables. There are these huge truths, and we're going to dramatize these truths so that the audience will understand them.

Once I know what the play is about, I begin to know what to see from the park bench where Joe Bonaparte is sitting. He knows he can make a lot of money if he sells out. So I'd sit him on the bench and have him see all of the rich people going by. There's a guy that drives by in a convertible with a beautiful woman sitting next to him. He's happy. He's laughing. Oh to be so happy. And there's a couple riding by on horses. Look how well dressed they are. Even the people sitting under the tree with a picnic have no worries. They have money. Life is easy for them. They have a butler serving the wine.

Do it out loud. This should be your preparation for rehearsals. Do it full voice. Get it out of your head. Don't whisper, don't play it under. Play the full character. Full voice.

You must elevate your mission as an actor. Expand your thinking, your frame of reference, and your understanding of the world we live in. And then pass along to the audience what you know. If the curtain goes down and the audience thinks, "Wow . . . that Cameron is one hell of an actor," then the play is a failure. If they leave thinking, "What a horror to give up what you love in order to survive," then the audience got the message.

There's an article in the *New York Times*, December 25, 2020, about what several singers felt was important about singing Handel's *Messiah*. A couple of them really hit home how a singer must also come up to the size of the theme. And, it's interesting, because I always think that singers often have these extraordinary melodies and a full orchestra behind them, so how hard can it be? Reginald Mobley, discussing the aria from *Messiah*, "He Was Despised," commented that what lay behind the song for him was an image of the Ferguson riots that followed the killing of Michael Brown. "I thought, I get to be a survivor and tell the story of my brothers, my sisters, who were scorned and shamed and spited and spat upon. And I have to carry that shame: of what Americans should feel allowing the system to go on as long as it has." Jonathan Woody discussing the aria "Why do the nations so furiously rage together" told the *Times* that behind the aria he was asking the people in the audience: "Why do we hate each other, mistrust each other, dehumanize each other?" On a lighter note, I sat in on a rehearsal of Mendelssohn's *Midsummer Night's Dream* with Dudamel conducting the LA Philharmonic and after their playing of the "Wedding March," I was desperate to run out and get married.

The more you "live" in the play's world, as you rehearse . . . the more you move into Joe and how he views the world, how he relates to it, and not only do you begin to "be" Joe, you grow as a person. You come up to the idea of the play. You grow as an actor with every play you do. And the reason that's true is because you expand your consciousness to a new level of understanding of the human condition.

Stop Pissing on Everything

As I think over the many ills that plague today's actor—playing clichés, making choices based on movies they've seen, making performance and line reading choices—one of the huge issues is we don't have a clear sense of the ideas. It's all very pedestrian.

Dear Mo,

This anecdote will give you an idea of the kind of mentality Stella Adler understood. In the early 1980s, years prior to the fall of the USSR, a Russian-Jewish film had made its way to New York. Unfortunately, I can't remember the name of it, but it was significant enough that I invited Stella to go with me to see it. As we were walking into the cinema, I asked her if she would like some popcorn or a drink or something. It was an absurd suggestion, I confess, since Stella Adler was hardly the sort of person to nurse a bag of popcorn, but I was slightly intimidated by taking her to a movie and I ever so easily could say something stupid. Stella looked at me firmly and said, "Darling, let's not eat while the actors are working."

Whether it was in a movie or on stage, Stella respected the importance of the actors' work and the occasion of the theater. Our legacy from Stella was to see the theater as a temple. And the classroom as well. It was always as if we were hearing the Beatitudes from the Sermon on the Mount—or more accurately the Ten Commandments from Mount Sinai.

In life we really do pull down everything. I have never ever heard someone say the Pledge of Allegiance and have any idea what they're saying. "I pledge allegiance to the flag of the United States of America." No one pledges allegiance . . . they don't even know what it means. There is no flag—or if there is, it means nothing. It has nothing behind it. No one died in a war. No one sacrificed and this is supposed to be a symbol of what they did. None exists. It's why I use the term "grocery list."

It's good for us in our everyday life to see the universal size of everything around us. Take a common everyday ordinary event, such as traffic stopping at a stoplight. Lift the event to a universal idea. The idea here is: "if you live in a civilization, you must abide by the rules." See it in a way that allows your mind to step back and see the larger idea behind the scene. You can use life knowledge to replenish yourself every single day. You learn something more about the human situation, mankind, the human soul, every single day and it is right there. Your material is in the world right now.

What this does is help you realize something about plays and the problems of characters. The problems of the human beings in the play. Every character that is written after 1860 isn't intended by the author to say something about human beings, because they are like the people in the audience. Joe Bonaparte in *Golden Boy* is not just that character: he is every character who wants to succeed and do something that kisses his soul, but he is caught in the struggle between "success and fame" and the longings of that soul. That's why Mr. Odets wrote the play.

Cameron: So . . . what you're saying in the traffic light example: in a civilized or complex society to say, the traffic stops, there are four lanes and it stops, you must enlarge what is called the actor's vision, which is necessarily larger than the fact. The fact if it just remains a fact is a bore. It is dead. But what you have to add is to take every fact and to raise it.

This is from Stella's class:

You are seduced in so many ways by your education and by not being stretched. Write this down: I must stretch myself. I must make myself able to play a part that demands strength. I must stretch myself. If not, you're cooked. You understand this stretch must go on every day. A woman walking with bundles out of a grocery store. What is large—universal—about that?

STUDENT: She wants to go home to cook dinner.
STELLA: NO! Don't invent plot.
STUDENT: Man is a consumer by nature.
STELLA: I don't think you're thinking about what she is doing.

You don't understand. What's large about that? Your soul is about this big. She needs to have the food for her life and family. All through the ages. Yes? You must understand that the theater, ideas, playwrights, parts are bigger than you are. You mustn't play your size because your size has already been mutilated. Is that clear? Your voice, your inability to see that life has in it humanity. Not with Shakespeare, not with fancy crowns, but the humanity of life is epic.

Don't pull it down. Don't make any plots. It is universal. It has gone on for hundreds of thousands of years.

Using the Theme—A Practical Application

In 2006, I directed a production of *Waiting for Lefty* in Seoul, Korea. The emails between Paul Lim and me (Paul played Joe) might help give you a picture of how knowing the theme can help an actor.

Dear Paul,

I absolutely believe that it is not possible for an actor to play a part without understanding what his character is going through. The next step in this is to move into Joe's view of the world. Keep in mind, the actor knows more than the character does. Joe doesn't know he's downtrodden, probably doesn't even know the word. He also doesn't know, at the moment it happens, that Edna is giving him strength. He's fighting for his life. I'm going to risk a sweeping generalization here . . . that none of us middle-class types have ever had to fight for our lives. The working class, farmers, peasants, refugees, immigrants . . . they all understand fighting for their lives. They have to do it every day.

But *survival* is an important theme. *The fight for life* is another important theme. You can't make little choices as an actor, when you know this is the idea behind your play.

There's an article on the front page of the *International Herald Tribune* this morning, with a large picture (and I'm assuming that it's on the front page of the *New York Times* as well): Jian Guohua, the Communist Party boss of Mianzhu (China), is on his knees in front of two women, who are holding pictures of their dead children. Imagine. Mothers were able to bring the Party bosses in China to their knees! Thousands of children lost their lives because of the "shoddy construction of public schools" ("government offices and more elite schools not far away survived the quake largely intact," *New York Times*, May 28, 2008). The article uses the phrase "they have overcome their usual caution about confronting Communist Party officials." One of the fathers in attendance, a quarry worker named Liu Lifu, grabbed the microphone and began calling for justice. His fifteen-year-old daughter, Liu Li, had died along with her entire class. "The people responsible for this should be brought here and have a bullet put in their head."

The Chinese parents had known for many years that the construction was bad. So had the officials. No one did anything about it—and now there are ten thousand dead children. The horrifying truth is that this is what it takes to get people to fight. But I think these are the people in *Waiting for Lefty*. They are people who have been pushed down this far. Joe's children are starving to death. When Edna tells him that she had to put the children to bed so that they wouldn't know that they were hungry, it's a moment when a fist hits Joe in the stomach.

There is no play that can be done without script analysis work that leads you to the theme of the play. Without this work, Marina will think that she's manipulating Joe. And Luno will think that, because—like the character he's playing—he has no money and has girlfriend problems, he's got the same problems that Sid does. It's not even remotely a play about not having money! It's a play about not having a life. Hopefully by analyzing a script in this manner an actor can get to the size of the play. Plays don't read well. Or, more accurately, they don't read with size. That's the actor's job. Every Shakespeare play has size built into it. I believe that it takes an actor with the size of Henry V to play Joe. ("Hold hard the breath and bend up every spirit/To his full height.") Shakespeare's words give it to the actor tenfold. The truth is, so do Odets's. Only it's bigger. Because no one in the audience of a Shakespeare play believes that the characters on stage are real. In Odets, we not only know these people, we are these people.

Dear Milton,

It can be so easy to dismiss a piece and think that we "get it" before really doing the work. Script analysis of a piece like Lefty, *a piece with—at first glance—simple concepts and characters, that comes to life only through such work. There were times in our discussions today that brought me close to tears. The size of the piece is astounding, representing all the people that have come before us, the ones that suffered and died to make this world what it is. I feel that we as human beings have forgotten these "real" heroes and have in a way turned our backs on the fights that they paid so much for to win. We have allowed the "money men" to take back what little ground they were forced to give up and have therefore taken their sacrifices and made them all in vain. None of the problems addressed in* Lefty *have been solved. Personally I think they have only gotten worse, made tolerable only through an increasingly distracting media and the realization that there are no simple answers. We no longer have the luxury of a fantasy as they did in the 1930s—the fantasy of a perfect system—and it has left us cynical, bitter, disillusioned, and without hope. In a time where the answers to all our questions are at our fingertips we have lost a sense of the quest for an answer. We want one now and if it is not immediately available we shrug our shoulders and turn our backs.*

Dear Paul,

One of the biggest issues facing actors today is their complete lack of relationship to the size of the ideas of plays. Writers are writing about huge, earth-shattering concepts . . . and actors today make everything very little. Very unimportant.

This lack of understanding of the size of ideas has led all of our acting to be pedestrian. We no longer can change the world. We merely entertain. People don't leave plays thinking about ideas, they leave wondering where to go for a hamburger. Or why they are having trouble getting good reception on their mobiles. As actors, if we truly understand the size of the ideas of a play, then we will make choices that support the idea. And if we can do that, not only will we be better actors, we will have more of an impact on civilization.

Realism: an ordinary man in an extraordinary conflict of the soul.

This is a phrase Stella used in Script Analysis. She used it to help us understand how huge the ideas are in plays. By "extraordinary," Stella means "larger than the normal turn of events"—the kind of torture that pulls a person in their life between unsolvable issues. And she used the word "soul" to help us understand we were not talking about an insignificant plot, but rather something deep.

In a play like *Golden Boy*, Joe Bonaparte is struggling between a life decision: satisfying his inner being—or making money. And he is aware he can't do both. In a play like *All My Sons*, Joe Keller—the father—had to struggle before the play begins. The plot: He had to decide between sending faulty airplane parts and saving his business . . . or not sending them and risk losing everything. But as a theme, the struggle between humanity and business. Big stuff, here.

Conflicts that call upon every ounce of ourselves to make a decision. Conflicts that have no logical basis for decision making. In other words, "Should I kill someone?" has a logical basis for a decision. "Should I follow my heart and possibly end up broke—or should I do something I'm good at, but don't like doing, and make a lot of money?" Decisions that are unspeakably difficult to make. And decisions that have no right answer.

Realizing this is helpful in making choices as an actor.

Knowing the theme sets you in the right frame of mind. Otherwise, you think Nora is "complaining" to her husband, Torvald, when she tells him that she went from living in her father's house and having her father's opinions to living in Torvald's house and having his. The play is terrifying when you realize the depth of the struggle for Nora to find a sense of herself. George Bernard Shaw once remarked, "When Nora slammed the door, it shook the world." That is not possible, if all she is doing is complaining.

In Realism, there is no solution to the problem. There is no easy answer to solve the problem of the play. There is no answer to what to do about Willy Loman. The world of traveling salesmen is a thing of the past. The world doesn't stand still. He's a flawed man in a flawed system. If Nora leaves her husband and children to go out into the world and find herself, will she be happy? Of course not. She left her family to do it. Even if she were to find herself, it cost her her family.

It's not so much that there's an answer in Shakespeare as there's an ending. Iago is bad. He will be tortured for his evil deeds. End of story. Hamlet dies. But he avenges his father's death. The lovers are reunited in *Midsummer Night's Dream*. It's very tidy. Also, and more importantly, none of these are real people and the plot is not real. We don't know people like Richard III. We certainly don't know people like Hamlet. None of our friends can say their uncle killed their father and married their mother. But in a play like *All My Sons* we can understand the characters' struggles. And the disturbing end of the play gives us no resolution. Kate says to her son, "Forget now. Live." But you know he can't.

It's why I like action movies. It's relaxing not to have to think. You know who's bad. You know who's good. You even know who's going to win. Sony Pictures Classics is my favorite movie studio, but I have to really be focused and concentrated to watch one of their films. Not only am I jealous the filmmakers got to make their film and get distribution, but their films make me think.

I suppose our job these days is more important than ever before. We must make people think. I'm afraid most people are like Joanne at the end of the second act of *Vanities*: "I've always found it's best *not* to think."

We have to wake people up.

6
Words of Warning

I'd Like Something That Works Every Time

Yes, who wouldn't?

Dear Karim,

The potentially frustrating truth about acting is that there are a seemingly endless number of ways to start work on a play. Like so many of us who have been educated in a system where we have been led to believe there is a right answer, I understand this need, but when it comes to the acting process, there is simply no right answer. Hopefully this will stimulate you rather than defeat you. My thought is this uniqueness of the possibility of an approach is what separates the children from the grownups.

Anthony Hopkins was asked about his process, and he said that he reads the script about a hundred times. Meryl Streep was asked about her process, and she said that she only reads it once and trusts that her impulses are correct and that her imagination will carry her through.

Just to make this clear: if you read it once, you won't be Meryl Streep and if you read it a hundred times, you won't be Anthony Hopkins. To quote my former colleague Joanne Linville: "If your talent is a room somewhere in your soul, there are many doors into it." The process we're exploring is clearly meant to help you find *your* road in. It makes sense that the road in is different for everyone, because our relationship to the world and life experiences are all different. And to add to that, it will be different for each part you do, because you will have a different relationship to each play.

May I suggest this as a frame of reference for looking at the text of a play: There is a world that exists—one that the playwright has invented. And in this world there are human beings who do or do not deal with their problems. It's almost a shortcut to ask, "What's my character's problem?" A play is really about this struggle a character has in the given circumstances of the play. If you don't understand and have a relationship with the world of the play, it makes sense you won't be able to have an in-depth relationship to the problems that exist with a character.

The work you've done on Quinn in Arthur Miller's play, *The American Clock*, has taken you on a path that has made sense. Certain issues about his profession hit you first. He's the president of General Electric, and it made sense that you needed to have a clear idea about that. Then the fact that the play takes place in the Depression became a factor, especially since he's resigning. Then you added in his past and events from the past that Mr. Miller has given us—and began to clarify how these events would shape his character. At one point you were able to add yet another area. What is his problem?

And the problems are *not plot problems*, but rather soul problems that give you a road into the *themes*. There are two distinct areas of exploration in acting. The ability to analyze a script—and the technique to do what you've analyzed. Merging script analysis with technique is the goal of a lifetime. Kazan had a great comment. "You need to be able to translate your psychological understanding into behavior." I would add to this any analytical or philosophical understanding has to be translated into behavior. There are all sorts of questions you can ask yourself to help clarify what you mean by "behavior": "And that makes me *do what*?" "That makes me *think what*?" "That makes me *respond how*?" "That makes me *behave how*?"

I agree. It can be frustrating because you have to be smart enough to analyze the text, but at the same time lose the logic when it comes to performance, lest it become antiseptic or accurate. A college essay.

We have a lot of tools. We use different ones with each play, with each world we enter. This is a good thing.

While not mechanical—and not mathematical—there are specific avenues to approaching a script. If you look at either Stella's book on Ibsen, Chekhov, and Strindberg, or her book on American writers, you can see how vast the possibilities are. The more you understand about the world the writer has created, the social circumstances if you will, the more you have as a basis for choices. Ysabel Clare approaches the idea as, "There is a secret world and we are leaking information."

Obviously you're not going to get it instantly. In fact it's the reason every actor I know looks back on parts from earlier in their lives and says, "Now I get it!" In the documentary dinner party I filmed with Eli Wallach and his wife, Anne Jackson, Anne talked about a monologue she had performed from the Shaw play, *Major Barbara*, as part of a fundraiser for the John Drew Theatre in East Hampton. The docu-dinner was in 2005. The play premiered on Broadway in the mid-1950s, and Anne had been the first Barbara. She explained to us at dinner, "Doing the monologue the other night was the first time I saw what Shaw was talking about. I really got it." We're talking about a monologue she had done fifty years earlier.

Don't demand of yourself that you get it right. It's the flaw in our educational system. We are taught to get it right, to get the right answer. It completely strangles the actor's talent. You must allow it to move slowly into your being. And if you get it wrong a few times, so be it.

You Won't Learn It All This Year—It Takes a While to Learn to Lie Well

It's always better to learn than to know. If you always know, you're in trouble.

—STELLA ADLER

Dear Teo,

There's an impatience in learning to act. It's frustrating because so often it makes sense but it's not working. And the worst part is, often when something finally makes sense, there's no clear reason why it happened, or why you missed it in the first place. I felt your pain when I passed by the rehearsal room and heard you scream, "Why is this so hard!"

Maybe the most freeing thing to admit about acting is that, in fact, *it's a lie*. You're not Nora, you're not Hamlet, you're not Kathy, Mary, or Joanne. The most simplistic definition of an acting technique is the process of making this lie appear to be the truth. Some people can lie immediately, like the time I told my father it was impossible I would be at a party where there was drinking. Some lies take rehearsal. Theresa definitely needed some work trying to explain why she was late to class.

Chris Carmack recently explained to me that his latest key to acting was that he did nothing. "Yes," he explained to me, "nothing. Then when I go out there if something happens, I know I've done enough preparation. If nothing happens, I know I haven't." He later added to this. "And I believe it."

The preparation. Oh my God. The tools that actors use. The craft. It's a lifetime of exploration, but in increments one begins to understand the elements. I point this out because I think it's important for an actor to understand that *you're not going to get it this year*. Stella once told that to an actress in my class and the poor girl looked absolutely crushed. You mean if I take this class with Stella Adler I'm not going to learn everything about acting? No.

Roberta Wallach tells a story about her father, Eli. She had watched him during the rehearsal process and early performances of a play that he was doing, *Visiting Mr. Green*. She went back to catch a performance about three months into the run in New York and was blown away. She went back afterward ecstatic to her father. "My God, Dad. That was beautiful. What happened?" Eli replied, "I finally got it." Roberta continued, "Finally got it! You've been acting for fifty years . . . and you finally got it!" Eli quickly corrected her, "No! Not acting! I got the moment that had thrown me."

My former student, Javi, loves to tell this story: Tallulah Bankhead was having violent sex with a famous director. Suddenly, the front door opens and in walks the director's wife. Tallulah twirls her head around and, without missing a beat, says, "It's a LIE!" Miss Bankhead was very experienced in her particular lie.

Try to relax into this process. This process of learning. The good news is that you will spend your lifetime trying to get it. At least you'll never be bored. There will always be a new discovery. And often the discovery will be something you already knew. Something that you've heard a million times, but all of a sudden one day it makes sense.

Not the Plot!!!

The plot will drown you if you rely on it as the basis for defining what's going on in a play or a scene—or what's going on with your character. It's an important element, but it's not the reason a character plays an action. A plot is not actable. What is actable is the relationship to the plot. The task you're doing is also not what's going on with your character. "I'm washing dishes" is not an action.

There is almost no moment in acting where there is not a danger we will answer questions with a plot. **What's happening to him?** "Well, he hasn't been making any money as a salesman." **"Why is she sitting in the dressing room?"** "She's waiting for her husband." **"Why does she always wear black?"** "She's in mourning for her life." The plot will give you essential information, it will certainly inform your choices, but you can't act plot.

> An email from Paul Lim:
>
> Drowning in plot was the term. And drown I did. I was literally choking in a labyrinth of unexplored impressions of what I thought to be a rich past. The fundamental oversight was the ignorance of the idea or conflict of the play, which was a man that felt he had to turn himself in for another man. Of course the stakes are high. To turn himself in does not just mean a few months in jail but almost certain death. At first glance there may be an enormous sense of dilemma or internal conflict but once further experienced there is not. To this man it makes perfect sense. The understanding and in turn the experiencing of the past of this man makes this make perfect sense . . . this is what gives the play a sense of nobility. For what is more noble than the truly willing sacrifice of oneself for another human being.

Every detail and choice must feed the play, otherwise take it out. It can only bring the play down and if you have too many of these stagnant details they will drown the piece (and the actor). In any case, do not allow the piece to become plot dependent. Make sure every choice and every word that comes out of your mouth is both relevant to and feeds the play. It must feed the play. Otherwise throw it out. You are adding fiction to fiction for no reason, when the whole point is to make the fiction real. As an actor the choices you make must be an attempt to ground the play into a reality.

There is no question it takes effort to get used to approaching plays without such reliance on plot. It is a daily occurrence when I ask an actor what's going on with a character, and the answer is invariably a recitation of the plot. The answer to the question, "What is going on with Willy Loman?" is not, "He just drove home early from a sales trip." Not only is that not actable, it's not particularly interesting. "He's losing his grip." As a stimulation for choices, there's no question a man losing a sense of himself is more stimulating than his sample bags are heavy.

I agree that finding the theme—or the idea—is often difficult, but I think we complicate it slightly. It's often about many things. And, often, in the realistic play different audience members walk away with different things. In *Death of a Salesman*, I might walk away thinking how difficult the relationship between fathers and sons is—and someone else might come away thinking it's awful what happens to people once they outlive their usefulness. Or even . . . my God . . . what a woman has to put up with during a marriage. As an actor, you need to be aware of all of these, even though certain themes will hit you more than others.

An important issue is for you to connect to the theme of the play in the depth of your being. You, the actor, must understand what you're saying. Call it the theme, maybe call it the idea. Maybe just decide when the curtain goes down at the end, "What do you want the audience to think?" Your choice for Biff Loman—that the pressure for success is strangling to young men today—gave you a center for all your actor choices. And the fact that you understood this so clearly added to the stakes of your choices.

If we begin to understand what our play is about, our choices reflect that. Certain techniques like wandering around with my character's life are good because they begin to help you get a total picture of your character in the world of the play. Stella: "Take your character three [or ten . . . or six . . . or nineteen] places *outside the play* and see how they live there—and then you'll begin to see how they live *in the play.*" The clearer I am on the theme of the play the more relevant my choices are going to be to feed this theme.

Stop Fiddling Around on Stage

There is an unfortunate habit actors get into of either wandering around the set aimlessly, leaning on the furniture, . . . or slouching on one leg. Even the cast of *Downton Abbey* (only the younger actors) were guilty of the same thing until the production's Historical Advisor worked with them.

> Dear Giancarlo,
>
> It's important that you're comfortable on stage, but you need to be aware that arbitrarily picking up props and playing with them not only gets in the way of feeding the action of the scene, it's distracting for the audience. Activities on stage are meant to feed the action of the scene, not just give you something to do so you feel comfortable. I once saw an actor in a class, whose need to be comfortable in the place knew no bounds, butter toast while telling his father that he loved him. While it's important to have a sense of all of the doable activities on a set, you really have to be clear about how doing them feeds your scene.
>
> Stella interrupted a student discussing nuclear power.

STUDENT: Nuclear power

STELLA: Stop! You are going to talk about nuclear power. Something that big and your hands are in your pocket. Nuclear. Power. You cannot hold your hands in your pocket. It's the habit of a child. It's hanging on. It's not letting go of the table.

I was your age and I had to walk down the stairs and it was an opening performance in Baltimore and I took the drape all the way down the stairs with me. You cannot hang on to anything. Don't stick your hands in your pockets. Don't look for change. Any big subject needs the character's size—not jingling. If you look at a symbol of authority like a judge, the judge wears a robe. There are no pockets. When the robe comes off the judge can put hands in a pocket because this is no longer a large character. Now here you are with a big point of view. Accept this and you will stop hanging on. Don't talk down, not so intimate with your voice. Reach out. I'm going to tell you something that must go into your heart. You must speak to the center of people.

A stage truth is: if I'm going to speak to you, I really mean it and I'm going to aim it at you. That's the difference between "I'm going to tell you something in a small voice." Aim at your partner. Strike the center of your partner. You can do it quietly. All this is not meant as criticism. I swear by my life it is meant for you to save yourself ten years of struggle, ten years in which you don't know where you're going. You say, "Oh, I'll be natural"—and then you're so natural that people say I'm bored. I'm not interested. You can choose what you want. But you can be absolutely silent with someone and reach them. Unless you're saying, "You gotta light?" But if you're talking about nuclear bombs . . . you must reach them.

She Likes Basketball

This morning I have been reflecting on your work and your acting. I also want you to consider acting and whether you want this as your life's work. My teacher, Stella Adler, once said to a group of actors, "You're at Step One. You want to be at Step Eight. You must go Two through Seven." I worry you think you can do this without putting in concentrated effort. I fear you think you can just throw the spaghetti on the wall and it will stick.

It's difficult for me to think of basketball without hearing Jerry Orbach singing the song "She Likes Basketball" from the musical *Promises, Promises*. It's such a joyful song that every morning when I hear the kid on the basketball court next to our office practicing, it makes me smile. I'm in awe of this kid, who comes in without fail every day to dribble and throw baskets. There's another kid, John, who plays the guitar. There is almost no time I walk through the halls of the college that I don't run into John practicing the guitar.

It's summer and as I think of my actors, I wonder if any of them have picked up a script, worked on an exercise, or even thought of going over something we worked on last year. My guitar player, John, certainly didn't "take a break" because school is out for the summer. As a teacher, it's up for grabs whether you can tell if an actor has real talent, but what is not up for grabs is being able to tell when an actor has been working on technique. If it's wrong, it's fixable. If it's right, it's earned. Bryce Dallas Howard was in my class at New York University. She did an assigned exercise early in the semester and then, after everyone had worked, she asked if she could do it again. She'd worked on it after comments in class. Bryce's work ethic is the reason she has a career. I would guess every teacher would find the same thing true. There are very few students who, once they've completed a class exercise, go back and rework it, either to make sure they understood why it worked—or to clarify why it didn't work.

Acting is big stuff, kids. The first actor appeared on stage over two thousand years ago. When you walk on stage you bring with you the two thousand years of actors who have gone before you. Stella loved the quote by the German philosopher Goethe, "I wish the stage were as narrow as the wire of a tightrope dancer so that no incompetent would dare step upon it." You have a responsibility to your art to treat it seriously. To rehearse. To come into class with thought-out, rehearsed work. If you think you're good enough to wing it and get by, then you need to go back to your high school. You can be cute and have energy there. We are preparing you for the big time here. You need to step up your game.

Just sayin'.

"Mood" Spelled Backward Is "Doom"

Playing an effect is another recipe for disaster. You get stuck with the idea of the response you want from the audience and play the effect, rather than the truth of the text.

Paraphrasing an editorial or a commencement speech is an excellent exercise for being able to get a clear idea of the sequence of thoughts, which is essential if we are to believe the play is not about the words. But, like all text, you don't want to play the mood of the thoughts.

Dear Greg,

Your second try at the Mark Donnelly editorial had a different problem. You chose a tone to play it. Creating a kind of mood of despair. The editorial starts with "I've been thinking about the German people in the early 1930s." This is something you must really be careful about. You decided in advance how you were going to play it. And because of that, I was more aware of *how* you were playing it, rather than what you were saying.

In fact, it made me think that you really hadn't been thinking about the German people in the early 1930s at all. What exactly were you thinking about them? What was the social circumstance of your play that made you compare Germany of the 1930s with America in 2019? What were people in Germany doing? What are people in America doing?

This is a perfect opportunity for you to talk out your thinking. Don't just answer the question! And don't *perform* your thinking. Own what you're talking about. In that scary play we did last year, *Good*, you had a frightening line, "Don't you think Germany is better without Jews?" Is this the thinking you're talking about in the editorial? What makes you think there's a similarity?

Also, be aware who your partner is. Who are you speaking to? What is your relationship to your partner? Let your partner give you your action. Your action can come out of the idea of why you're telling us this. Are you trying to wake us up? Or maybe the impulse for the editorial is, "I'm at a loss what we're to do." It could even be, "Get off your asses!" It could be any number of things, but the point is that it has to be clear. This will help you avoid the tendency to play a tone of despair.

This is an important concept in acting. Yes, you might be in despair, but if you play the mood of despair, we are going to get some general idea of despair. Whereas, if you play an action, if you have a clear idea what the impulse is for telling us in the first place, you will have something specific to grab on to—and the effect will take care of itself.

Also, make sure when you're working, you don't just work in your head, but work out loud. Talk out everything while you're driving. Let it go. Let the argument go where it wants to go. I think the problem with the monologue this time, is that you're so set on how to play it, you've lost the life of the acting.

7

Thoughts on Building a Character

What You Do Is Who You Are

All actor decisions must be turned into behavior. Keep in mind that acting is not like one of those cartoons where there's a bubble over the character's head that explains what's going on. A character trait is a scary term for many actors. If it makes it easier, think of it as the character's personality. But there is a truth that someone walks into the subway, and you think "what a jerk"—you need to ask yourself "why?" you think that. The answer is because of their behavior. Character is based on what someone does.

Dear JP,

The character in the Tracy Letts play, *Killer Joe*, is not just a stretch for you, it's out there in another world. It's an excellent opportunity for us to explore exactly how you access a character so far removed from yourself.

The research you did by looking on YouTube to find similar type characters was extremely valuable. At least now we know what these characters look like and how they appear on the outside. It also allows you to move into the first stage of work on character. Best described as *imitating* what the character is doing. How they sound. Their physicality. An attitude. Exercising this muscle is a great start, even though it's not the ultimate aim. I would take it, however, over the clichés and indications that we normally get with these characters. When *Vanities* was running, Jack Heifner and I would drop in on productions around the country. You cannot even imagine the Texas accents we had to deal with. Even in Dallas, which is where act 2 takes place.

The ultimate goal is to move beyond the imitation stage to the stage where you inhabit the character. I keep going back to the undercover Federal Bureau of Investigation agent who, on the morning of a sting, would dress like his invented character, talk like him, talk about things he would talk about. The lie became the truth. The fiction was defictionalized. You develop this ongoing monologue where you talk about all of the things that are a part of his world. Simple things. What you hate, what you love, what you find scary, what thrills you . . . on and on and on. Working your way into the thinking of your character.

Working this way, you have a clear relationship to how he sees the world and how he lives in it. You begin to own it so we're not sure where you stop and the character begins. Importantly, the lines come out of your understanding of character.

You begin to live in the place and let that life feed your character as well. I was watching an episode of *A Million Little Things* last week and I was astounded watching Christina Moses in the kitchen of her restaurant. The confidence with the use of the props and place blew me away. I started watching *Grey's Anatomy* because my former student, Chris Carmack, has a recurring part as the new orthopedist. Very clear work with the procedures, absolute confidence about what he was doing. Mind you, I had a knee replacement last March and as impressed as I am with his abilities in the operating room, I think it's pretty clear I wouldn't have let him get near my knee with a scalpel. But, the point is, you have all of these possibilities to help you. And the way your guy responds to his circumstances tells you a lot.

Part of your talent as an actor is the ability to choose what you need in order to make your character believable. In the case of the

Tracy Letts script, the biggest element for you is the class of the character. Trailer park trash. Very difficult for someone with a degree from Rutgers, but not impossible. Actors clearly do this kind of work all the time. Petrovski had to both learn Russian phonetically (after assuring them when he got the job that he spoke Russian) and learn the accent. Years ago Grant Show did an afterschool special I produced and when we hired him, I asked him if he could ride a horse. His answer was epic and I bought it, "I'm from northern California. Of course, I can ride a horse." Two days later as I was jogging in Central Park I noted someone getting a horseback riding lesson. As I passed Grant, I muttered something like, "I never saw this!"

I had a funny experience earlier today. One of my closest friends is a day trader (a stock market term, apparently). By mistake Ken sent a text to me. (Yes, I know. It's your worst nightmare.) His text read, "So what are we thinking SPX does the rest of the day. ES is at 2931 right now. Did you hear that Xi said he's willing to sit down again? I think the DOW could get over 500 today. How do I get preference and access to shorting BYND when shares are slim?" What hit me while reading this text, because I have no knowledge whatsoever of the stock market, was what I would have to do to play this part. There are actors who would just memorize the words and say them. It's another thing that separates brilliant actors from day players. They are the ones who are absolutely clear about everything they say onstage.

Getting to the thinking of any character is essential. You are right to suggest that you should find activities he might do during the day. The more you daydream your character in all sorts of places, the clearer you will be about his life. Shop for these choices as well. Put him in a place where it's difficult for him. Another place where he's got it together. Give him a task that he successfully figures out. Another where he fails. All of these things help get to the idea of how he sees and lives in his world.

The transition from imitating a character to inhabiting him is sometimes difficult, sometimes not so difficult. Peter Brook says that once in a generation we have an actor who is the incarnation of the part. Well, at least we know where we're headed.

Everything Already Happened

There is no present without a past. Building the past is one of the great joys of acting. It's the perfect use of improvisation . . . improvising monologues to justify the facts of the past. Stanislavsky called them **études**. An étude where you improvise a scene from the past, which is not in the play, *and* with a scene partner, gives you a solid relationship to both your partner and to the text. Simply said: building the past gives you ownership of the present.

The importance of building the past doesn't just give believability to the present, it gives you an impulse for the scene you're playing. All of the actions that explain the character take place before the curtain is up. What you bring onto the stage is the character's continuation.

Dear Teo,

You are absolutely correct. None of the actors—*not one*—bothered to build the past in the Donald Margulies play, *Long Lost*, we saw Saturday. I was really horrified from the very first line of the play. Two actors merely reciting lines as if that were all you needed to do. There was absolutely no sense they were brothers or that they had a stormy past. There was certainly no hint that they had not seen each other in years.

The facts of this particular play, particularly noticeable because they were missing in the actors' work, bring up another demand on the actor. You must have a sense of the price you must pay in order to earn what the playwright has given you. "My brother was doing drugs and caught our house on fire—and killed our parents" is huge. I don't remember a play with such a huge fact to be dealt with. As an actor, you absolutely have to know what it takes to make that plot point truthful. Just saying it certainly doesn't make it true. I can't repeat enough: part of your talent is the ability to tell the difference between the size of a fact like "my brother caught the house on fire and killed my parents" and one as insignificant as "you drank a six-pack of beer yesterday." Having a solid technique gives you the tools to build both.

There's a play that already exists by the time you get to "lights up." What happens onstage is a continuation of what has already happened. In the Margulies play it's as if the actors waited until it was explained in the script for the news to surface. From the first scene, we should have sensed there was something wrong and then when we find out what it is, we say, "Ah . . . that explains it."

It's the reason we spend so much time building the past. The étude you and Jesse did when you were working on *Death of a Salesman* was one of the best examples of building a past that I've seen. Biff giving Happy tips on going out on his first date. The two of you were so clear about your characters and your relationship with each other that I wanted the scene to be in the play. And, of course, when you got to the line in the bedroom scene, "You taught me everything I know about women," it was true. You had paid the price for the experience of the line.

I'm still furious about the Donald Margulies play we saw. Without having too much of an attitude about this, I notice from their bios, all four actors have done a lot of television. You can tell. In television, you're hired because you're a type they're looking for and so damned

often you just rush to a performance, which involves intelligently playing the words. That never works in the theater.

Dear Wesley,

Excellent session today. And you can see how subtly the past
is built into the script, and how important it is for the entire audition
scene to own that past. Your guy only has a couple of lines that give
you the entire past of the character, and if you don't build those in
a very experiential way, you miss the entire spine of the scene. The
world is filled with those actors who say anything, thinking because
they've said it, it's true—and there's nothing behind it. I know you
would give up acting before you became one of those actors.

"You get that I was in juvie for auto theft, right?" And then when
he finds out she stole the car: "but actually stealing cars? That nearly
ruined my life."

We live in such a great time. The fact we could so quickly find
two fantastic documentaries on YouTube about kids in jail. Keep in
mind, this is the difference between an actor and someone who just
does intelligent line readings. Any actor can decide in advance how to
say a line like "That nearly ruined my life," but almost none have done
the work to figure out what that means. David Krasner pointed out a
moment to me in *On the Waterfront*. Brando has a moment when he
tells Eva Marie Saint he grew up in "some home." You know everything
about his childhood from those two words. We should know absolutely everything about your character's experience from the sentence,
"That nearly ruined my life."

You must own that past or the scene is just a collection of lines.
It's so interesting how easily the scene falls into place when you are

aware of the past. Why is the girl so important to him? Why is he so upset by what she's done? It all makes sense.

We briefly talked about the use of the future, and it's interesting how that helped. What is the positive outcome for the character? He will stay out of jail and pull his life back together. What is the negative possibility? He will end up back in jail. Knowing this negative possibility gives all of his actions stakes . . . an urgency.

And, as always, when you work on the past, don't do it in your head and certainly don't write it down—do it out loud as a little monologue. And be specific. When we're working in class, I suggest if it helps you get to that specificity, start with "there was the time that" or "I remember one time." It's helpful in fighting the tendency to be general.

Good work.

The Play Starts in the Past

Dear JP and Chris,

Without a clear sense of the past you're doomed with a play like O'Neill's *Beyond the Horizon*. In every play you walk into the room/ onto the stage with your past, but in this one if it's not in your bones and blood, you will look like two farm boys on a national tour of *Oklahoma!* Especially if you assume that because it takes place on a farm, they must have Texas accents. (The play takes place on the east coast in 1918.) It's the reason we still haven't done a reading of the scene. We just don't know enough yet.

When Stanislavsky passed on to Stella his ideas about the given circumstances of a play, they included all of the elements necessary to make characters in a circumstance believable. The past walks on stage with them, or in the case of Robert, it exists when the curtain goes up. In the televised version we could only watch for forty-five seconds because it was so bad, the actors decided to do a clichéd idea of "brothers" and there was no past at all. In the opening scene of the play, the brothers are saying goodbye to each other before Robert leaves on a three-year ocean voyage with their uncle. If you don't have a sense of what it was like to have someone leave home for three years—a hundred years ago—then there's no play.

The Imaginary Line with a Past—Ysabel Clare's Timeline

The importance of the past cannot be overstated. You can almost think of it as, "Everything has already happened and then we have a play." The opportunity to build this past is part of the great joy of being an actor.

Dear Chris,

Vintage Stella Adler: "There is no present without a past." "The present exists to prove the past."

For me the question in *building the past* has always been a bit of a muddle between building the actual past—as if you are living in that moment, or do you build the past from the perspective of the present of the play?—looking back on when it happened.

When I was beginning script analysis, I took Stella's advice and underlined every line with a past. Some were extremely obvious as in the scene between Chris and Ann from *All My Sons*. "You remember, overseas, I was in command of a company: . . . Well, I lost them." As an actor, it goes without saying that you must build that. On the other hand, the relationship between Chris and Ann and their past is not talked about very much. Even so, it has to exist or you have no play.

Then the journey is to come up with shared moments in the past . . . moments that are borne out of the text of the play.

I have toyed with various aspects of "how do you best build a past?" I've had some extremely strong études done in class that come to mind. Anson and Charles, while working on a scene between Prior and Louis in *Angels in America*, built their second date (an example of something not in the play). Teo and Jesse improvised a scene where Biff prepares Happy for his first date (also, not in the play *Death of a Salesman*). Clay did a remarkable improvisation where he built a past of a kid who was molested, a scene which was talked about in the play, but because he couldn't go there by talking about it, he physicalized his character with the walls closing in on him.

As always, we get back to the same conclusion: there are no rules in acting, but we are always looking for some kind of methodology to help us access this lack of rules.

At the Stanislavsky seminar I attended in Prague, I met a wonderful teacher named Ysable Clare. In a discussion about building the past of the character, she said she had her students draw an imaginary timeline on the floor, where they would identify the present, the past, and even the future. They would then walk to a place in the past and step on the timeline to build the moment they were after.

I found it very freeing—Ysabel Clare's suggestion of a **timeline** for the character. The actor draws an imaginary line on the floor. "Here is the present. Down there is the past. Up there is the future." You can actually "see" the life of your character in front of you.

I have no idea why having an imaginary line of the floor is so freeing, but it really is. Maybe it's because we've seen so many time-travel movies—we get to play in one. Having the timeline in front of you had another benefit. Oddly enough, it had a benefit of allowing you to stand outside the line and analyze, philosophize, come up with psychological reasons for behavior . . . all of the thinking we do (and often over-thinking) while figuring out what about the past is necessary and relevant. Ysabel suggested all of this is fair game while standing outside the timeline and viewing it. But once you step onto the timeline, you are there . . . in the moment you are building. You enter the character's world. Your imagination work is there for you, your relationship to other characters, the images are in front of you. The many and various elements of your technique are available to you. But you are really there for that moment. Then you step back off the timeline and you're back to you.

We've been experimenting with this concept in class since I returned. All my actors have loved it—and one of the more interesting aspects is something Ysabel suggested would happen. When you step off the timeline, you breathe a sigh of relief. There's something about physically stepping onto an imaginary timeline that is exhausting. You can't do it for very long.

Peter had a major actor breakthrough doing this exercise. Peter comes from training that encouraged him to over-analyze, over-think, and worst of all, write endless pages of backstory. When we first met, he told me he'd written something like seventy pages of backstory for a James McLure play called *Private Wars*. Without knowing it, all this academic work was crippling his talent. He knew so much, he could quickly answer any questions about his character. The problem was that there was no life in his work at all. His work made sense, it had a logic, certainly it was justified, but it had no life to it. He was the incarnation of another Stella bumper sticker, "Facts are death to the actor until they are fed through the imagination and become the experience of the facts."

Peter had begun work on a play called *The Boys of Winter*. Playing a doctor, testifying on behalf of a soldier accused of killing women and children during a raid in Vietnam. From his research on the Vietnam War, he was able to choose a moment from the past that spoke to his relationship to the young soldier. The payoff for all his research was that he was able to choose a truly meaningful moment from the past to build. He stepped onto the timeline and began to experience totally a moment when he saw the racist white soldier holding his dying black buddy in his arms. Although he talked about the moment in the past tense, it didn't matter, he was there. He stepped off the timeline, slightly overwhelmed with what had just happened, and as Ysabel suggested would happen . . . he all but collapsed from the experience. I then told him to move back up to the present and improvise the monologue. It was, quite honestly, breathtaking. There was a stunned silence in the classroom.

In fact, his having so fully experienced the past of the character, the action simply appeared. An example of how the past can give you the action of the scene. I think this will be valuable for any actor, but for an actor like Peter who has a tendency to explain everything within an inch of his life, it temporarily liberated his talent.

Tim made an extraordinary choice in his work playing the father in the Caryl Churchill play *A Number*. It's indicated in the script that when his son was four years old he gave him up to the welfare system. Tim chose to improvise talking to the child, telling him why he was giving him up "even though I know you don't understand what I'm saying." He then followed it up with another improvisation, where he was trying to convince the hospital administration to let him keep the two-year-old clone of his first son. Both exercises were remarkable in giving life and depth to facts in the play.

Ysabel's timeline is a great gift. So much of acting can be so heady and elusive, but having the past right there on the floor seems to liberate actors. I owe her.

Emotional Recall—Or "If You Can't Play the Moment, Just Make It about You"

I'm not sure why it ever made sense to substitute your own life for the character's life, but somehow it worked its way into a methodology of acting. "Hamlet's a guy like me" may seem like a joke, but any number of actors approach the play as if their relationship to the world is similar to Hamlet's, and they can use themselves. It's usually not as extreme as that, but it rears its ugly head under the umbrella of, "My girlfriend left me. I'll think about that during this moment and it will make me cry."

Dear Greg,

It's probably a good time to revisit my thoughts on the use of emotional recall, especially since I was up all night thinking about the question you asked at the end of class yesterday regarding your confusions about it.

Although Stanislavsky used emotional recall early in his teaching, he eventually abandoned it. There's a question as to why he would have used it in the first place. Although there are rumors to the contrary, I'm not old enough to have asked Stanislavsky, but I can surmise it was a part of his lifelong quest to discover something almost impossible to figure out: what is the nature of the creative process? I would hazard a guess it was also born out of the form of theater that would change the world in the late 1800s. Realism. For the first time in the history of the theater, there were human beings on stage. Human beings on stage with real, recognizable, human problems. These were not plays about a man who killed his father and married his mother, but plays about three sisters who were immobile and unable to move forward with their lives. Like real people.

The fact that there were human beings on stage demanded a new way to approach acting. Merely standing and having a clarity about the words and the sentences was not enough. There was something beneath the words. And it was the job of the actor to address not just the question "What am I talking about?" but more importantly "What's really going on in the scene?"

Emotional recall was no doubt born out of Stanislavsky's need to understand human behavior. While it might make sense that one would need to understand the emotional moments of a human being's life in order to get to an emotional moment in a play, it didn't work out so simply.

One of Stanislavsky's translators is Jean Benedetti. In his book *Stanislavski: An Introduction*, he talks about the problem Stanislavsky had with emotional recall and the reason he would eventually abandon it. "The result can be an introverted form of acting." The actor will pull the play into his own experience rather than using his own experience as a tool for a more thorough understanding of the meaning of the play. Sure, it could give the desired "effect," but it wasn't the play. Benedetti notes that in the hands of star players it can produce charismatic results, but "used by lesser talents the result can often be self-indulgent and stultifying. It was precisely these lesser talents, however, that the System was designed to help." When Josh Logan asked about emotional recall as a technique, Stanislavsky answered,

"I don't know what you're talking about. Oh no, no, no. That's for the beginning, for the bathroom or the middle of the woods, where you can be alone. You must never use it when acting; it's a means to an end."

Another issue is a side effect of pulling the play down to your own experience. Mr. Stanislavsky found that when actors used their own lives to achieve a moment in a play, they would invariably shy away from the moment as they approached it. It's like you're rocking along and then you can see it coming and you really don't want to go there. Do you really want to relive the moment you discovered your lover was cheating on you? The image that comes to mind for me is skiing up to the edge of a cliff. Obviously, if an actor shies away from a moment because they fear going over the cliff, then any misbegotten "effect" hoped for is destroyed.

Marie Danvers reminded me of another problem, one she encountered. Marie starred for a year as Maria in a European tour of *West Side Story*. In the moment where Chino comes to tell Maria that Tony, the boy she loves, has killed her brother, the director told Marie he wanted her to cry. In order to satisfy that moment, Marie, because of her training at the time, thought about her father dying. She confessed that every time she used her father's death, it took her out of the play.

Because of the tendency actors have to decide in advance how to play something, the use of emotional recall feeds right into playing an effect as opposed to the truth of the play. It's as if you're saying, "I know . . . I'll be really sad here," and then you relive something that made you sad. Or, the usual . . . "I think I'll cry here." Or the director wants you to cry (always a bad choice). So you go back to the death of your dog and it makes you sad and you cry. Whereas if you build experientially the truth of the play, and your performance comes out of that, it is the stuff of great acting. Playing an effect is almost always lumbered with the horror of clichés and the limitations of your own life. The inability of a character to deal with the given circumstances of a play is the stuff of great drama. Playing the effect you think might exist really undermines the play.

The biggest problem for me is that the use of emotional recall pulls the play down to the level of the actor, rather than helping the actor come up to the size of the play. And by "size of the play," I mean the size of the idea. This is where we get little actors, using their little lives as the basis for huge plays. Or, as Stella Adler once admonished an actress, "Darling, if we wait for you to find an action in your paltry life, we'll be here all night."

There are given circumstances to any play. The facts of a play get you to thinking. Perhaps the thinking stage involves your experience, maybe it doesn't. As soon as you start to think, "I wonder what it's like to be at war and lose your men?" then the work has begun. Slowly letting these thoughts wander around in your being, you begin to open up. You begin to understand the experience of what the playwright is giving you. You begin to inhabit the character and his world. It takes time. Stanislavsky says you should daydream your character in his world. Slowly the line between you and the character begins to disappear. You enter the character's world for a time. You see things the way your character does. You respond the way he does—and then you leave it behind. (And when you go home, you don't have to scream at your girlfriend.)

Problems from your life that send you to some emotional place? Well . . . that's why you go to therapy. To deal with it and move on.

Me, Myself, and I

The confusion about using your own life seems to be one of the crucial issues of misunderstanding. The use of your own life while doing a play is a constant source of confusion for actors. Do you use it? Don't you use it? I have several emails about this question. This is one of the first ones I received.

From Cameron:

Ok right, so when you were a kid playing war, you imagined the circumstances and believed you were a soldier, but YOUR soldier was different to another boy's soldier because naturally, your brain is made up differently so you interpret the character of the soldier differently?

Yes, Cameron. That is exactly the case. Every actor will approach the work on a part differently. My background, because my father was in World War II and had told me stories, would definitely be different from Bobby's, whose father was secretly gay and told him completely different stories. Petrovski, on the other hand, had no direct relationship with anyone he knew being a soldier, but his personal relationship with the idea of friendship was clearly at work when he made his choice for the beginning work on Chris' monologue in *All My Sons*.

It would be very difficult to eliminate who you are as a person from any of your work. The issue to trust here is that while your own life experiences may feed your choices, it has nothing to do with using your own life experiences instead of the play's. Don't confuse having "you" in your work with substituting the play's circumstances with your own.

For instance, I did a monologue about this boy talking about his mum and where he grew up, etc., and was told to imagine my own backyard when I was a kid, and the tutor said that my connection was better when I did this.

I'm sure your connection was better . . . but being connected is not the only issue. You want to be connected from the point of view of the character in the world of the play he's in. It's dangerous and stupid. It's like saying I connect better with Jenna than I do with Lorna (in *Golden Boy*), so I'm going to relate to Jenna and not the play that Mr. Odets has given me. Again . . . forcing the play to be about you, not about the character in the given circumstances of the play. You may be able to connect better to your own backyard than Central Park, but that's one step away from saying (and I've heard this said—and done—before), "I know this monologue is about Edmund's relationship to the sea, but I think of it more as my relation to having an orgasm, so I'm playing the monologue as if I'm having sex."

The actor process is not just about *making it work*. This approach to acting feels like it's for an actor who wants to get away with it. "Ha! Fooled 'em. They thought I was in Central Park in the 1930s, but I was in my mother's backyard." The focus is wrong. You're playing a desired effect (apparently in this case the effect is to be comfortable), instead of what the play might be after.

Your teacher is applauding the idea that you're connecting, leaving out the fact that it had nothing to do with the play. No wonder there are so many bad actors in the world. Or perhaps he doesn't think it matters, as long as you're connected. Or perhaps he doesn't know what the play's about, which is certainly a possibility. Or perhaps he's just a bad teacher, which is highly likely.

The work of an actor, and the goal of the technique, is to give you tools that will allow you to experience the world of the play from your character's point of view. It's a world that is imagined by the playwright and we have a responsibility to bring it to life. Your tutor's thinking is the reason we no longer have big actors capable of playing big parts. This need for a shortcut in order to act without having to do the work is criminal.

Your question leads me to bring up one of Stella's biggest points: as an actor you have to understand the theme of the play from your inner being. I know that sounds like a pretentious thing to say, but your relationship to this theme will inform all of your choices. This comes up in class time and time again. When I ask you what a play is about, the answer is not the plot. It's about the universal idea behind the play and the more you grow as a person, the more depth you will bring to your work.

That's what you're really after. Choices that feed the theme of the play. Your own life will help you, although certainly there are instances outside your frame of reference. At a Q&A for the movie *Fences*, Viola Davis confessed when she was on Broadway performing the play, there was a moment she could never get. She could never understand why her character was so desperate to have her husband's illegitimate child in her life. She explained her frustration, "My God, I thought, I went to Juilliard. I can do this." But she said she never really got it. By the time she did the movie, she'd had a child of her own and it was absolutely clear. Mind you, she won a Tony Award for the play and an Oscar for the film.

But It Happened! To Me!

There's a great moment in the film version of *Who's Afraid of Virginia Woolf?* when Elizabeth Taylor disdainfully brays at her guests an imitation of her husband, "But it happened . . . TO ME!" I always think of that when an actor relates something about the justification for making a bad choice, as if the fact it actually happened to the actor makes it good theater.

Dear Tony,

I know, you saw it and it was your real backdoor and your real street and you once ran for the bus on it, but, because you didn't create it in a way that fed you, you had no connection to it except that "I saw it" and "it happened to me." As a result, it was completely uninteresting. Edward did the same thing yesterday. He started with "Every Saturday I take my dog to the park." He got about as far as "dog," before I lost interest. And even though I'm impressed Noah can go back to the death of his favorite pet and cry every time, I wonder about a concept of acting that encourages you to be in a backyard in Ohio in 1948 and then suddenly decide "I think I'll cry here"—and mentally rush off to a veterinarian's office in Jackson Hole, Wyoming, in 2016.

It's a very big, arguable point about acting—the use of your own life. And not just in making choices, but also in substituting your own life and experiences for that of the play's given circumstances. In the annals of theater history, it has been a continual battle. It was not only the basis for the conflict between Stella Adler and Lee Strasberg, I've now attended two international symposiums on Stanislavsky and it continues to be discussed eighty years after Stanislavsky's death . . . thirty-five years after the death of Strasberg . . . and twenty-five years after the death of Stella.

So where did that lead us? In today's class, both Tony and Edward fell prey to a mis-assumption about acting: if it's real, it's acting. Similarly, if you can see it, then it's real, and therefore it's acting.

What's interesting is when I asked Edward to describe the street where he lives, he began to immediately select elements of the street to feed what a horrible street it is. Complete with parking meters so you can only park for an hour, as well as the darkness of the street from the trees along the pavement. When I asked Edward to repeat the exercise, he went even further in depth, lending truth to the idea that each time you go back to something there's the opportunity to go deeper into it. Repeating the description didn't deaden him, it gave him the opportunity to dig further to find what stimulated him. The key, therefore, has to do with making choices that bring you to life. I'm talking about this as if it's easily done, but when you are not interested in what you're talking about, you can hardly expect us (the audience) to be. When Edward very specifically built the street where he lives, everything fed him—and none of us will ever visit him.

Edward even admitted he was bored by his dog in the park. I can only ask, "Then why choose it?" Part of the talent of being an actor is in your choices. And you must always be aware that your choices must activate you. Must bring you to life. Must ignite you. Otherwise, you will be a blob on the stage.

If you need a back door, why would you go to your back door, when there are doors on structures in Florence that are a thousand years old? Why go to your dog park when there are dog parks on the beach at sunset? Why go to your job and suffer that misery when there are Jewish slaves building the pyramids for the Egyptians? Tony and Edward's exercise put us to sleep; JP's exercise, where he screamed, "I hate my job," scared us to death.

Although I never discussed it with Stanislavsky, I'm sure he would agree the other problem with using your own life is it becomes some-thing you use to get an effect. I was horrified once while watching an acting class to hear the teacher say to this really, really sweet woman, "I want you to do the scene again and think of someone you really hate." I looked at this warm, cuddly woman and could not imagine she could ever hate anyone . . . much less use that person instead of the partner in front of her.

Can't Stop Responding as Me

From Michelle: In the scene where Beckett gets angry with Dierdre, I can't stop reacting the way that I would in a situation like that. I cry and I hide. I'm not doing it from her character at all. It's really frustrating and I don't really know how to stop from just being me.

As Sharon Carnicke pointed out in my conversation with her about this problem, Michael Chekhov had three areas for us to see the difference between you and your character: physically, emotionally, and the will of the character. But I think we can add to that and be more specific.

Start by asking: "How do I handle myself in tense situations and how does Dierdre handle herself in tense situations?" You've told us how you handle yourself: you breakdown and cry. A totally different response for Dierdre, in a tense situation: she buckles down and stays focused. She won't back down.

The danger here is that you understand it intellectually, but not as a behavior. And that's when I suggest you ask yourself, "Like when?" And take a mental, "There was the time that . . ."

This is an extension of the idea that you take your character outside the play and see how she lives there, and then bring her back in. When it comes to trying to see how Dierdre deals with seemingly tense situations, take something much smaller to start. You know where you're headed, but starting at that point would probably be overwhelming, so start small and build on it. Keep in mind Stella's axiom: "I can believe this much today."

Something smaller. A less important event. An altercation with the florist. "I said I didn't like red carnations in the bouquet. Would you please take them out?" And the florist yells at you that it's your fault. "You weren't clear what you wanted." There's a pause and Dierdre says, "I'd like you to take the carnations out of the bouquet. Now! And I'm going to wait. Either that or I'm not going to pay for them and I will go elsewhere."

So in the tense situation, Dierdre focuses in on the problem that exists right now. She controls the problem and solves it. Building her almost as a second person, talking out this étude, you begin to see how she behaves in a situation where somebody is yelling at her. When someone is yelling at you, you cry and shut down, whereas Dierdre arches, gets stronger, and gets clear.

Also, if you don't feel comfortable using the first person right away, then don't. If you can't say, "I stopped the florist and took control of the situation," then say, "Dierdre stops the florist and takes control. She tells him . . ." This is me being a broken record, because it's such a consistent problem with actors, but keep in mind, "The way you say it, is the way you'll do it." You are not *reporting* what she's doing, you're *experiencing* it.

Come up with several of these situations, any situation you can believe, and it will help you begin to own her behavior. "I pull into a parking place and there's a woman who decides that it was going to be her parking place, even though she was on the other side of the barrier. The woman gets hysterical. 'Miss, the parking place is mine. Please stop yelling. I don't have time for your nonsense.'" Dierdre unemotionally focuses in and solves the issue. And if you do these little études out loud, you begin see the world from her point of view. You begin to own her in that situation. Now going to Samuel Beckett is not so daunting.

"Mr. Beckett? Are you finished? You can either talk about this with me or you can let readers believe all the rumors."

She controls the situation. Also, we know the end of the story. He does tell her what she needs to know. She has a logic he cannot fight.

Yeah, talking it out that way is very helpful because it just moves me out of myself now.

It's a very common issue where an actor responds to the play's circumstance the way they would respond to it, rather than how the character would. Greg did it when he was going off on the lack of involvement of the members of the Mattachine Society. But it was more Greg's frustration with people like that than his character's. And, obviously, Raphaël's response to the Nazi war criminals at the Nuremberg Trials was more difficult to sort out, because he and his character might have closely related responses, but Raphaël lost control, which is something you never want to do on stage.

The Good Kind of Fill-in-the-Blanks

Deb Margolin starts all of her classes with fill-in-the-blanks. A fill-in-the-blank is simply the beginning of a sentence, which the actor (or playwright) finishes. They're brilliant. Used at the beginning of a class, they get you to focus on yourself. She also uses them to help actors and playwrights explore a character. You finish the sentence as your character. In fact, I started using fill-in-the-blanks with actors as a preparation for a performance. It's brilliant for getting you to focus in on your character. It's also extremely helpful to use a fill-in-the-blank as the first line of a one-minute (or whatever) monologue from your character's point of view. I have hundreds of them, but it's a good idea to develop the ability to write your own. To get you started, here's a bunch.

- I envy people who
- Once in a while I
- I find it strange how
- The softest part of me
- I think continually of
- My imagination is most active when
- I am shy about
- My aggression gets stimulated when
- I often suppress
- I hate to be required to
- I often find myself looking
- I have never
- The hardest thing for me to learn
- I feel connected
- My past sometimes
- My daily life is narrated in a voice that is
- My knowledge and my faith diverge at the point of
- I'm naturally
- The thing I love about my family is
- The thing I hate about my family is
- People don't talk enough about

- The thing I don't get about daily life is
- In the dark I
- I remember
- I've forgotten
- How soothing it is to
- I am constantly bewildered by
- I have already tried and failed to
- I cry whenever
- I want to
- In my mind I go over and over
- I do and do not want to talk about
- Because I want it so badly, I'm terrified of
- I'm unsure of
- I hate that I
- I'm a sucker for
- I'm never more alive than when
- I keep waiting for
- I've lost
- The oldest anger I feel has to do with
- Sometimes I worry about

How Do You Get to Experiences You Haven't Had?

You have lived everyone's life. You just haven't gotten around to it yet.

—Stella Adler

The joy of acting as far as I'm concerned is how it allows you to expand your own horizons.

Dear Edward,

This is a curious question coming from you, since you've played many different kinds of parts. Think about it, most plays are about experiences we haven't had. I'm guessing you were never a stoner in a pub in Camden Town, the character you played in that incredible Che Walker play, *Been So Long*.

It was either Stephen Sondheim or Ernest Hemingway—or maybe it was Stephen Sondheim quoting Ernest Hemingway—who suggested the creative impulses come from three places: experience, observation, and imagination. It was suggested you must have two of these, one is not enough. I would suggest you must always have imagination no matter what. Experience and the power of observation added on to the imagination will allow you to explore an encyclopedic number of choices. Even if you do have experience, I would not eliminate observation. After all, someone else's experience might be better than yours.

What you lack in experience, you make up in observation. There are a couple of types of observation, one of them being research. We live in such a remarkable time, I feel as if Google, YouTube, and countless documentaries on every subject give us open access to almost all available research.

Kevin Bacon was working on a part once: the convict in *Murder in the First*. His research was extremely complete, and he said to me at one point, "You should tell your students to watch documentaries, so they can see what the real people are like." It was a brilliant suggestion, and you will note the number of documentaries I use in my teaching. Although *Band of Brothers* is one of the best series ever on television, it's nothing compared to the truth of characters you get in a documentary like *Restrepo*.

I think this is one of the biggest flaws in today's actors. Their frame of reference is extremely limited and most often based on films they've seen. When Chris Petrovski was playing the Russian spy Dimitri on the television series *Madam Secretary*, the episode where he was released from a Russian prison, his director, Eric Stoltz, encouraged him to do research. He was very specific with him, however. He told him he was not to watch prison movies. He could watch documentaries or read books, but not to go to Hollywood movies for his research. Chris chose to read (much of) the Aleksandr Solzhenitsyn book *The Gulag Archipelago*. I say "much of," because the book is almost two thousand pages long. I'm certain he found enough for *Madam Secretary* by page 156 in volume two. It's a beautiful moment when Dimitri gets out of the car to walk across the bridge between Russia and Finland (in White Plains, New York). And most interestingly there are no lines, but you understand completely the hell he's been through.

I can't resist relating this story, because of its absurdity. Jesse was in a film not too long ago and he reported that an actor very excitedly confided in him, "I imitated Will Smith from a scene in *Fresh Prince of Bel-Air*." When an actor uses a movie reference (or worse, a television reference) he is condemning himself to a scary mediocrity. We all steal; the trick is to steal well. Stella said to an actor once, bravely doing a scene from *Streetcar*, "Darling, don't steal Brando. Steal what Marlon stole."

Reading about something or watching documentaries, or even better interviewing someone in the play's world is really useful. It allows you to guide your performance more toward your impulses. When my mother was alive I used to call her constantly to ask her about life during the Depression. You get so many keys about the way people see their world and how they live in it . . . or lived in it in the past when they're the real deal.

There are so many elements of acting that boil down to whether you have an actor's instinct. You have to both know what you need and then trust when you've got it. You develop the ability to know what information applies to whatever text you're working on. Sometimes it takes more digging than other times.

The first time I met Michelle was when JP brought her over to my apartment because she was having an actor-in-panic moment. She was playing the part of a woman who desperately wanted a child. Michelle was completely lost. Way too young to consider why someone would want a child, much less understanding why someone would be obsessed with it. Her teacher had erroneously suggested to her that she think of something she wanted really badly and substitute that for the desire to have a child. For totally understandable reasons her desire for an Apple MacBook Pro was not useful in her attempt to find the desire for a child.

Stella encouraged us to explore "the nature of" the facts of a play. What is the nature of motherhood? What is the nature of that need to have a child? What is the nature of a parental connection to a child? When I suggested to her this would have been the road I thought would have been more useful, she got it immediately. As if by divine intervention, my next subway ride was filled with mothers and their children. On their way to the park perhaps. The museum of natural history. It didn't matter. You saw the joy of a mother reading to her daughter as they road to their destination. And the smile of delight on her daughter's face. Who wouldn't want that!

It is important as an actor that you become a participant in life— and not an unconscious observer who wanders through with no relationship at all to the world you're in. We are not other people. There are numerous abilities necessary to become an actor, especially if you want to become an actor with depth, an actor who makes genuinely gifted choices. As soon as I saw the mothers on the subway, I knew exactly what the nature of the love of a mother was. The joy in both the child and the mother gave it to me.

JP asked a similar question when we were working on the opening scene of *Beyond the Horizon*. How do you get to an experience you've never had, like saying goodbye to someone who will be gone for three years? Especially when the play takes place in 1918. What is the nature of saying goodbye? And especially early in the last century when you weren't sure even when you would hear from the person again. JP likened it to a death. What happens to the person left behind when someone dies? The person who has left is no longer any place you always saw them. It is something we could use. Something to hold on to. Saying goodbye was knowing that you would no longer see your brother in any of the places where he used to be.

There's no question the process changes from play to play . . . from script to script. Very few performances are as riveting as Eddie Redmayne's portrayal of Stephen Hawking in *The Theory of Everything* or Elbe Wegener in *The Danish Girl*. Obviously there are different explorations when you play someone with ALS and when you play a man transitioning into being a woman. The issue here is mostly a trust in your choices. Second-guessing yourself is one of the biggest stumbling blocks we have to get over. The constant wondering if you got it right. *There is no "right"!* There is only *your* right. And it's *your right* when you make a choice that you love. When you make a choice that stimulates you, **and it makes sense in terms of the play**, that's what acting is about. Yeah, I know. Easier said than done, but it's the direction you want to head in.

You Are Not Alone

Clarity about your partner and your relationship to the partner frees you up as an actor.

Dear Victoria,

One of the joys of acting is you know where you're headed when you start the scene. You don't just wander out and hope you will bump into an action. And, because the play has defined the world you're in, you can make choices to feed into that world. Having a partner is a godsend to help you get there. Your partner gives you both the obstacles and the focus to get where you're going.

When Patrick Stewart was playing Prospero in *The Tempest*, even though I'm sure he was exaggerating to make a point, he said all he knew when he went out is that Miranda would be there and then the play would take care of itself. Like I said, definitely an exaggeration, but he was smart enough to know the forward motion of the play was dependent on responding to his daughter.

Chris Petrovski had a funny experience on his first episode of *Madam Secretary*. He was so prepared, so clear what he was doing, so certain of what his action was and who his character was that after the first rehearsal of the scene, Tim Daly very patiently turned to Chris and said, "Hey, Chris. There are two of us here."

To the cast of *Time Stands Still*: My note from last night's performance is to the entire cast: You're not the only one on stage. You talk because you're responding to what someone else has said. Or because of something that's happened. Otherwise you wouldn't have said anything. I'm not really getting that these are people who have a relationship with each other. Don't let all your preparation exclude your partner.

It made last night's performance seemed rushed. I felt like at times there were four soloists on stage and not an ensemble. And that each of these soloists wanted to get their part heard as efficiently as possible. You need to be clear that your reason for talking is in response to something your partner says or does. In a couple of instances, I felt like I was hearing a monologue.

Also, you need to be careful Jenna that the exchange with Mandy doesn't sound like "this is the theme of the play." Be clear you're responding to the fact that she does not understand why you do not involve yourself in the subjects you are photographing.

Same thing, Victoria. Don't let the monologue about the little elephant sound like a monologue. Be clear you're trying to get her to understand why you think what she does is morally wrong. You're saying, "It doesn't make sense to me how anyone could just stand there and do nothing." It's why she has a problem with "bummer" articles in the newspaper. She can't read depressing articles because it makes her want to do something, but she doesn't know what to do.

Make sure, Peter, you are really responding to the fact that they are planning to return to the war zone. It was a little bit too much like, here's where I have an outburst. Just be clear, Noah, what you're saying. I need to really know how wonderful it's been to cook and watch Netflix, as opposed to your former life, which involved worrying that tomorrow you might get blown up. Otherwise we won't get the disturbing realization in the play that people grow apart and what brought them together in the first place no longer exists.

For tonight's performance I would like all of you to work on concentration more. Develop the ability to enhance this muscle. Decide to really take in the world around you. Discover everything. Richard, what specifically do you see in the pictures on the laptop? James, what physical sign in the way Sarah walks gives you a hint she might be in pain? Even the rotten food in the refrigerator has to be clear for you to say you left so fast you didn't throw anything out. Sarah, how does Jamie look at you that makes you know he's being over-protective? When Jamie talks about giving it all up, what do you really see? Is it everything all those guys said to you before you met Jamie? Mandy, there's something people do—probably a look they give you—which you happen to misinterpret and it encourages you to keep talking. What is that look? You will apparently talk about anything endlessly. Genocide is about the only thing that will stop you.

So many actions you play come from responding to your partner. Be very aware of your partner; let your partner tell you what to do.

8
Thoughts on Playing Actions

Actions Not Words

When I'm sitting in a play and I'm miserable from watching some actor's bad performance, my most common criticism is that the actor isn't playing an action. I may have other criticisms, but if an actor is mindlessly saying words and sentences, it's a bore.

Dear Raphaël,

You are making sense out of your monologue and your ability to connect to what you're talking about is extremely strong, but what's missing is a thread to pull it all together. A clear sense of what your character is actually saying. It might be helpful for you to explore why he's talking about this.

When my former student, Sam Marks, returned from the Moscow Art Theatre he shared with me a great piece of information he'd learned. "A play exists on two levels: first, there's, 'What am I talking about?' And then more importantly there's, 'What is really going on?'" The **what is really going on** is a great way to look at what we're talking about when we refer to the action of a scene.

I understand the confusion about the concept of **actions**, but it's worth the struggle to understand it. When you're clear what's going on in a scene, it completely frees you up as an actor. You can really let go. You saw what happened to Taylor in the experiment we tried in class the other day. She was given a mundane piece of dialogue, but playing the same line of dialogue with five different actions was a revelation. That's what it looks like when an actor is clear about what she's saying and what's behind the text. The clarity of knowing what she was talking about really freed her up and she made some kick-ass choices. She really opened up and came to life.

The ultimate aim here is to figure out what's going on with your character in the given circumstances of the play. There is a reason your character does what he does or says what he says. It's the thread that pulls everything together.

I cannot repeat enough, **the way you say the action is the way you'll do the action.** It's not about the words you use. You're not a writer, so the vocabulary is not the issue. And you're not just reporting the action or answering the question correctly. You are looking for the experiential relationship to the action.

> The traditional method of stating an action is the infinitive form of an active verb. The action is simply stated: "to ____(active verb)____."

As with every choice you make in acting, you are looking for a choice that stimulates you. As much as I'm more concerned about your relationship to what you're saying than the actual words themselves, it is true that finding the right word is a great key. You're looking for a word that brings you to life. A word that gives you one of those, "That's it!" moments.

Shop around for your choice. Philip Seymour Hoffman was talking to a group of us and commented that sometimes he has a general idea what he's looking for and then uses a thesaurus to find the right word. I loved that idea. Obviously someone else did, because there's a book out called *Actions: The Actors' Thesaurus*. I use this idea of actions often when I'm directing. I was working with an actor on a monologue from *Death of a Salesman* when Biff tells Willy that "we're a dime a dozen." The action "to confront my father" didn't do anything for him. The thesaurus suggested "take on" as a replacement for "confront." It worked beautifully. "To take on my father." Great action. Really helped him with the scene. He completely came to life.

Over the years of teaching and directing, however, I've found that limiting yourself to this one way to access an action can make you both frustrated and a very sterile actor. Despite the attempt to avoid merely reporting your actions, I see actors all the time approaching their actions as if it were a guessing game or a recitation of facts. Greg did it the other day. He stated, "I think his action is to break free of his past," as if he were answering a question on a quiz.

The important issue here is that every acting choice you make must bring you to life. If you're merely reporting something, it's not going to bring you to life. In fact, it may bore you to death. Here's another bumper sticker for you: If you make a boring choice, you're going to be boring.

Also, keep in mind, no one is testing you on this. The object is not to get it right. If you are playing Irina in *Three Sisters* and you choose the action "to hold on for dear life" when you hear Tusenbach has been killed, no one is going to stop you at the stage door to either ask you what your action was . . . or disagree with your choice. The action comes out of your in-depth understanding of the circumstances of your play.

Realizing how the traditional approach to actions may not "ignite your talent," as Stella would say, I'll suggest some other inroads that might help you access the action of the scene.

- Ask yourself: "Why am I going out on stage" (or more specifically, why are you going to whatever room or space it is)? As long as you don't answer with a plot, it's a strong way to find your action. "Why am I going out on stage?" If your answer is, "To blast him out of the water," it will give you the impulse you need. It's not a plot. It's an emotional impulse.

- Another example of trying to find that impulse came when I was working with Teo on a Shaw monologue. When I asked him, "Why are you telling us this?" the result initially was a confused explanation of the plot. So I re-worded it: I asked him, "What are you saying to us?" He replied, "Wake up, people!" That worked. You need to be able to find something that activates an impulse that works for you.

- The first line in the second scene of the Odets play *Waiting for Lefty*, is "Where's all the furniture, honey?" I can't tell you how many times I've heard an actor do that line as if he were merely curious why there was no furniture in the house. Talk about not understanding what is going on with the character! In Korea, when I asked Paul what was going on with Joe in the scene, he responded with heartbreaking pain, "Life isn't working out." When he said the line, you knew it was true. He didn't just answer the question, he was a man losing control of his life. It was the exact action he needed for the scene.

- Just to add to this, when I used to coach Kyra Sedgwick on movies, she suggested we label each scene. It was one of the first times I realized how freeing it was to to "label" scenes with playable actions. "This is the scene where I let Mom have it." "This is the scene where I beg for forgiveness." All she needed was this clear impulse for a scene. And because she had such a clear relationship with everything she was talking about, she really flew.

A note about wording an action: The cardinal rule is, "Never use 'to be' when playing an action" ("to be sad" "to be outraged" "to be sexy"). Another variation of this is, "I think she's sad here" or "I think he's outraged in this scene." "He's being sexy here." So . . . what happens when you do that? You "play" an idea of sad or outraged or sexy. Directors have exacerbated the problem by giving actors notes such as "make him edgier," "soften her up a bit," "I think he's really pissed off in this scene," etc. Wesley said he recently received a direction in an audition, "Make it funny." And my favorite will always be when a director told Sigourney Weaver, "Do it again. The same way. But massage it a little."

Whether it's the actor deciding the effect they want or the director giving an actor an effect, it inevitably leads to indicating and playing clichés. Save yourself by turning the direction (or your own thought) into a playable action. If the director says, "I think he's angry here," rather than pushing a performance of anger, translate the moment into an action. "Blast him out of the water" comes to mind.

This is an important concept to understand about acting. You have to find your own road in. I don't really like the idea of insisting on some kind of quick fix idea of getting to the essence of a scene. "What do you want?" may seem innocent, but it dangerously can lead you to a very superficial answer. And one that drives me crazy is, "What do you want your partner to feel?" It may appear to be a logical question, but if you're not careful your answer will be way too tepid. You really cannot approach acting as if it's some sort of outline to fill in. Or that if you answer the question correctly, you can play the part.

As long as I'm on the subject of potential landmines, I'd like to add that writing out all the actions before you start rehearsals makes no sense. The actions are born out of the character's problem(s), so you don't want to rush the discovery that allows your understanding of the character's problems to grow in depth. It's fine to make a note in your script, but you also have to be able to erase it as your character evolves. And just a slightly bitchy note about acting teachers: to have actors write out actions in the margins and turn them in makes no sense at all.

I would be remiss if I did not include what for me was the absolutely monumental discovery I made when I read an article by Sharon Carnicke about translating Stanislavsky. Stanislavsky used the Russian word *zadacha* as part of his exploration of a character and the character's world. The translation of the word as Stanislavsky defined it is "problem." The logic is clear. Stanislavsky was suggesting to us that every character has a problem. Obviously, if you have a problem you want to solve it. And the way you solve it is through the action of the scene. It saved Paul during rehearsals of *Waiting for Lefty*. When I asked him what Joe's problem was, his answer, "I can't make life work," was the *zadacha* (the problem) he needed to find an impulse for the scene.

While I'm on the subject of *zadacha*, it's as good a time as any to bring up one of the biggest missteps in the study of Stanislavsky (also discussed in the Carnicke article). The English translation of the first Stanislavsky book, *An Actor Prepares*, was done by Elizabeth Hapgood, who was not actually an actress. She was a Russian scholar. For reasons that defy explanation she chose to translate *zadacha* as "objective." Not "problem" . . . "objective"! There is no similarity between these words as far as I can see, but "objective" has clearly lasted as part of the vocabulary. There are so many concepts that are thrown into acting that confuse and complicate the process. Trying to figure out an objective is one of those complicated areas. It's not even a great word, because it has built into it the possibility of failure. I've never liked the word.

From the standpoint of clarity alone, "what's your character's problem?" is much more accessible than "what's your character's objective?" If someone asks me what my character's objective is, I think I'd freeze in the headlights, but I understand clearly the idea of a problem. What Stanislavsky was saying was that every character has a problem. Whether they have an objective is way too heady for me to make it actable. And just in case you're with a Russian purest, yes there are other translations of *zadacha*, but in the context Stanislavsky used the word, it's clear he meant "problem."

When you're trying to find the action of a scene, you should leave yourself open to whatever helps. Last night coaching JP, sometimes he would use one form ("to clear the air") and other times he would use another form ("Grow up, dude"). The basic idea here is, "I am looking for the road in—to what is going on in the scene." Like many actors, JP has a tendency to set line readings, a result of having much too much reliance on the words and sentences. By playing an action, it both kept him from doing line readings and freed him up to be more spontaneous.

Hi Milton,

I was thinking back on your explanation of actions and the discussion about the actor who played Joe in your production of Waiting for Lefty *in Korea. You asked him what was going on with Joe and he said, "I can't make life work!" You agreed that "I can't make life work!" was a playable action. So, in order for "I can't make life work!" to become his action I assume it was loaded with the inner life from the*

struggle or problem that arose out of the circumstances in this scene.
Since he had already worked on the past, the relationships, etc., does
that mean you can only truly find the action once you've taken all these
things in? Only once you've truly understood the character's problem?

Dear Cameron,

The more you begin to understand the character and take in the character's problems, the more depth you will have with what's going on in the scene, and therefore what you are playing in the scene. And by "playing," I mean the action of the scene and not some effect you are after. I have a feeling that what's built into your question is an attempt to figure out if there is some kind of running order for how to play a part. Well, yes and no is my answer. Even if you do a lot of analytical table work before you get up on your feet, you will find that rehearsals are a new period and the discoveries you make cannot be set before you start. They are ever evolving.

And, yes, you're quite correct, Cameron. The action comes from the character's perspective. Building a character in depth is an ongoing process of discovery. And it's vital to understand that the action will change as you dig deeper into the world of the play. This is an important idea to take in: you can't set in stone anything connected with acting. The more you rehearse, the more you work on something, presumably the more depth you have. And with this depth will come changes. All sorts of changes. Particularly with the way you play an action. It is the reason Stanislavsky as a director stopped blocking his plays. He understood that all stage movement should come out of the character's relationship to the action of the play. It also makes sense that the more you grow in depth, your relationship to your world will change.

I mention this time and time again, you have to allow for the changes that come from the growth in a part. You cannot marry what your initial decisions might be. The analysis is ongoing during the rehearsal process. It's not as if you can analyze the script and then perform it. The more you work on a script, the more insight you get, and it's almost as if you end up going back and analyzing it again. That's why you should never say to a director, "But yesterday you said . . ." That was yesterday, we knew much less yesterday than we do today.

Do You Put an Action on Every Line?

Cameron: If I understand correctly, once you've found that focus and confidence in the scene, through playing this overall action, you don't have to worry about playing different actions on every line because your being alive in the scene will take care of finding these colors and different approaches on the individual lines, which all feed into the action and attempt to solve the problem.

I am hesitant to ever think there is anything you don't have to worry about when it comes to acting, but I have found that having a specific relationship with everything you talk about is essential to becoming alive in the scene. Think how often you hear an actor playing a monologue all in one tone. (Think Mel Gibson and his speech to the troops in *Braveheart*.) The action may be clear, but the lack of a specific relationship to every element gives it a sameness, which makes it tedious.

Willie Loman's world is falling apart. He's losing his grip and cannot pull his life back together. All of that is useful in deciding what's going on at the beginning of the play. But as an actor you need to have a specific relationship to everything you talk about that has happened. In the first half page of dialogue alone, there is a world of experiences that need to be specific. "I came back." "I'm tired to the death." "I couldn't make it." "I suddenly couldn't drive any more. The car kept going off on to the shoulder." "I came back ten miles an hour. It took me nearly four hours from Yonkers." The specific relationship to each of these gives a performance the colors you need. It's not a grocery list of all the things that happened. Each one of these has a specific life to it.

Ellen was paraphrasing a commencement speech in class the other day, originally given by Cory Booker to a Yale graduating class. The speech starts with a reference to a group of kids who used to play in the lobby of his building. Ellen was absolutely clear what the thrust of the speech was, but it was not until she got specific with the visual images of the lobby and the kids that the depth of the action appeared. The eventual death of one of those kids was built into her first words. The action clearly came out of her specific relationship to the facts of the piece.

In 1914, Yevgeny Vakhtangov, a famous teacher at the Moscow Art Theatre, remarked, "An actor, at every given minute, must believe in the importance of what happens onstage." Said another way, "Everything is something." There are no throwaways. No unimportant details that you slide through. If you approach the text as having importance, and you're clear about your relationship to what you're talking about (and you don't push it!), the colors take care of themselves.

While I understand the idea of putting an action on every line, it not only never worked for me, I found it stifles most actors. First they're trying to find the right word and then once they find it, they're trying to remember what word they picked, which totally defeats the purpose of having an action. It also seems dry and way too academic for me. One of the reasons I decided we need to broaden our view of actions is because it's too difficult to find a vocabulary that really brings us to life. Not that it doesn't exist, it's just hard to find. It always seems to me we're guessing what the action might be as if it's a test question on an exam. Hardly the most creative environment for work.

Stella's edict, "The way you say the action is the way you'll do the action," really is at the bottom of all of it. That's why I think we need to liberate ourselves from the overwhelmingly constricted vocabulary of acting. Stanislavsky never wanted that. Sharon Carnicke, in her article about translating Stanislavsky, writes, "Simplicity of description was Stanislavsky's stated objective." Stanislavsky was never looking for a be-all and end-all vocabulary of acting. He was trying to base his usage on common words. Actors are getting bogged down by a vocabulary of acting that never was meant to exist.

Cameron: This action, coming from the immediate circumstance, will probably change as soon as the circumstance changes (which could technically happen within the same scene?), but I assume you found this action for the entire scene or does that depend?

Not only *could* the action change in a scene, it *will* change in a scene. That's actually what does happen in a scene. A scene is a sequence of actions. Hell, an action can change from offstage to onstage. Your action to go onstage could be to shake some truth into him . . . and then when you arrive, you see him in tears and your action changes immediately.

Don't let the word "action" scare you. It's the reason that I will often use the word "impulse" instead of action. There's an impulse that takes you onstage. Be brave. Believe Stanislavsky: don't be crippled by the vocabulary of acting. If it's easier for you to ask yourself "why" you're doing something, then use that. Don't let yourself be stopped because you felt obligated to ask yourself, "What's my action?"

With these questions that you would ask yourself, like "Why am I going out there?" is that similar to asking, "What do I want?" Because if I answer, "I want him to give me my twenty dollars back," then the next question is, "What do I do in order to get what I want?," right?

The plot is important, but it's not an actable reason for why "I'm going out there." Here's where I think we get bogged down with all these damned questions. If I ask the question, "What do I want?" and I answer with yet another plot point, then I'm further complicating it because I have no choice but to ask, "What do I do in order to get what I want?" If it works for you and you blow us out of the water, then by all means. But in my mind, it adds an unnecessary bump and also can easily lead to yet another plot answer. "I want him to give me my twenty dollars back" is a plot. Much more stimulating to an actor is answering the question "Why am I going out there?" with an action. Something along the lines of: "to slaughter the bastard" or "to get to the bottom of this" or "to tell it like it is" . . . it could be one of a thousand different things depending on your play. It's active without over-complicating matters.

The point is I am looking for a playable impulse. Starting my work with asking, "What do I want?" and then having to follow it with "What do I do in order to get what I want?" forces me to add an extra step. It also leads me to over-thinking, which I always find crippling. The answer to how do I get what I want, when my reason for going out is to get twenty dollars back, also leaves me open to a tepid answer. I can imagine the answer to "How do I get what I want?" being stated in some mushy manner, like "by reasoning with him." But, hey, sometimes you have to go down that road first. No harm in that at all . . . as long as you find an impulse to take you on stage that feeds you. (And, of course, an impulse that's appropriate to the play you're in.)

Fight . . . fight . . . fight thinking what you're merely looking for is the answer to a question. Talk it out. If it brings you to life, then you're on the right track. It's all meant to ignite your talent. Make sure that it does. Also, fight thinking that once you've found something in rehearsal, you're going to do the same thing every day. You must give yourself permission to grow and change as you know more about your character in the given circumstances of the play.

The choice you make has to fill you as an actor. If it stops, then you have to revisit your choice and add to it—or change it. One of the reasons it's so difficult to write about any of this is because I need to hear you say it. It's not just about the right words, the right phrases, the right choice of actions . . . it is about how you say it. How it affects you.

You must experience everything. Carnicke says she thinks "experiencing" was the most important concept of Stanislavsky. When Stella said "facts are death to the actor until they're fed through the imagination and become the experience of the facts," she was talking about something that goes through every ounce of acting. It's the reason merely choosing a good action is not enough. You have to experience it. The reason I began to suggest other roads to finding an action is because the traditional vocabulary was not bringing actors to life. Actors would either explain, analyze, or philosophize about what was going on. And it deadened everything.

9
Reflections on the Process

A Very Good Place to Start

"When you sing you begin with 'do-re-mi.'" When you act you begin with . . . oh dear. Where do you begin?—Is there a very good place to start?

Dear Kaleb,

If there were anyplace I consistently start, it would be with the author and the title. As my former colleague Chris Thornton used to say, "Knowing who the author is tells you which cloud you're under." I suppose with many writers, "cloud" is the right word. Knowing your play is by Arthur Miller immediately gives you a mindset that is consistent with Arthur Miller plays. A second place I use as a start is the title. *Death of a Salesman* is something of a spoiler. You know when you read the title Willy Loman will be dead by the end of the play.

Keep in mind, all of the facts of the given circumstances exist to stimulate your creativity. It is not just about answering the question correctly or being able to write an essay on the subject, although I do believe when an actor is thoroughly prepared for a part, a master's degree in the subject is an understatement. Karim has been working on the Arthur Miller play *The American Clock* and week by week, he has not only become an expert on the Depression era, he knows about the success of corporations during that period.

Although it's difficult in film and television, since who the hell knows who writes *NCIS: Los Angeles*, but you certainly know the genre you're in. Often in character breakdowns they give you pieces of information you can hold on to. In film, you can certainly have a sense of the style of the director. In an interview with Christoph Waltz, who took a script analysis class with Stella Adler, he said that having studied Ibsen with Stella, he followed her lead and began with the playwright. When he knew he was auditioning for a Quentin Tarantino film, he sat down and watched all of his films. It obviously worked, since he won an Oscar for his performance in *Inglourious Basterds*.

Different ideas hit you at different times with different parts. It also is different with every actor. Matt was a history major, so he will often start with the social moment in history. Certainly different from where you would start, since that's not your area of interest. I've been working with JP on a monologue and the first thing that hit him with this particular monologue (from the Donald Margulies play *Sight Unseen*) was that it was a monologue about art. Good. That's where we started. A lengthy discussion about what is art. About the commercialization of art. The randomness of it. When we moved into an étude, improvising the sequence of thoughts in the piece, everything was based on his understanding of the idea of art, and his choices all fell out of that understanding.

So many exercises that we do are meant to help you live off the given circumstances: the place, the plot, the props, the period of the play and all that includes, your partner, the profession of your character, the past of the character, the character's point of view. Everything that is in the world of the play. All of these elements are there to help you begin to fill in what can stimulate you as an actor.

Writers create a world in order to say what they want to say. No matter how you start, you must understand the world the playwright has given you. You could never come up with choices in a scene without knowing who these people are and how they experience the world they're in. What their frame of reference is. Their morality. Ideas about family, marriage, friendship. In class and in rehearsals we have the luxury of spending time on understanding the writer's world. You will be ahead of the game when you are able to do this on your own.

Slow and Steady Wins the Race—Don't Take It All on at Once

The facts of the play and the understanding of how these facts will help you make actor choices is one of the joys of slowly reading the text and taking in all of the elements of the play. But at the same time, you can't let it overwhelm you. I hate those thousand-piece puzzles, because it's hard to believe that somewhere in the pile on the floor there's the Tower of London. I fear acting is a little like that and if you're not careful you'll implode.

Dear JP,

I hate to say it's true, but slow and steady wins the race. You're not suddenly going to have this huge revelation that solves everything. It can be frustrating until you embrace this idea.

Keep fighting your tendency to take on half a dozen big facts of a play all at the same time. That came up in class with *All My Sons*. Yes he's a commander, yes the men in his platoon were killed, yes it's World War II, yes there was one particular soldier, but if you build it all at the same time, you're going to frustrate yourself. It's not only overwhelming, you're not fully exploring experientially every fact along the way.

I could see it happening to you yesterday. You were working on one fact and before you had fully let it land, you were distracted by another fact. It's not that you shouldn't move on to another fact, but I keep thinking you're mentally shrieking, "Oh, my God!" before every new fact. It's great that your creative impulses are free associating, but don't get defeated by them. I blame this habit on our educational system. It becomes like cramming for an exam. This is all symptomatic of a need to get every answer as soon as possible.

Start Slowly—It's Your First Time Reading the Script!

There is a space between the written page and the actor. The space is diminished by the actor understanding the meaning of the words. The result is an idea.

Dear JP,

I want you to be very clear about what you did yesterday. You really need to bust yourself on this. While we were working on *A Prayer for My Daughter*, you leapt so quickly to the words "Vietnam" and "there's a woman inside me," it completely threw off the meaning of the monologue. Just because the word Vietnam is in the text doesn't mean it's a guy suffering from post-traumatic stress disorder—anymore than "there's a woman inside me" means he's transgender.

In script analysis, this initial period is called impressions. In other words, you are not worrying about the performance; you are not even worrying about the choices. All you are doing is letting whatever happens occur to you while reading. It might be the plot, it might be the characters, it might be the way the characters talk—short sentences, bad grammar, big vocabulary, two characters obviously not listening to each other . . . the point is, it could be anything. It might be the playwright. Perhaps the city where it takes place. Allow what hits you to hit you. It's the first step and you should not be rushing to make performance decisions. Let these pieces of information simmer around.

And there's really no right answer. There are some specific roads in to your work, but so much of your work has to do with you. Think of it as your road to ownership. Akende made a huge breakthrough when he asked the question about a character, "Why does it matter to him?" As he began to answer the question, he developed an entire relationship with his daughter. Suddenly he came to life and so did his relationship to her.

Think of this work as switching on a light in a darkened room, it is a process where you discover what you have to work with. What you find in the room cannot overwhelm you. There's a line in a Stephen Sondheim musical about the painter Georges Seurat, which I have completely paraphrased. He says more or less to the audience as he begins to paint, "A blank canvas. My favorite. So many possibilities." Every play is filled with possibilities. Don't limit yourself by either jumping to a conclusion too quickly or taking the first thought that comes along.

Anything can help your road in.

Does the Writer Know as Much as I Know?

Working in depth on a play takes the knowledge of someone getting a master's degree on any topic. An actor doesn't just know the facts of the play—there is deep-down understanding of what these facts mean experientially. It's easy to wonder if the author knew all this information while writing. This question was sent to me after we'd spent an entire class on the opening stage direction of a Clifford Odets play. I love this quote as a note to screenwriters from "Adventures in the Screen Trade," by William Goldman. "The screenwriter doesn't have to know why the hero dives into the river to save the drowning dog. All he has to know is that he does." Unfortunately, the actor does have to know why.

Dear Wesley,

Although I think Mr. Odets' process as a writer is quite similar to ours, he has one job, we have another. Writers write the text. That's their contribution. Ours is the interpretation of the text. We have the insurmountably enormous job of filling the space between the words and what becomes the performance. Stella: "The words are the author's contribution. Bringing them to life is yours."

Stella once told me that Arthur Miller demanded that Lee J. Cobb audition for the role of Willy Loman in the original production of *Death of a Salesman*. Kazan wanted him for the part, but Miller didn't see it. It seems impossible now. The video of Cobb's performance exists and when you watch it, he is overwhelming in the part. Compared to Dustin Hoffman, Philip Seymour Hoffman, and certainly Brian Dennehy, Mr. Cobb wipes them across the floor. It seemed impossible to me that this story was true, but several years ago I ran into Arthur Miller's sister the brilliant actress Joan Copeland, at a party in East Hampton. I asked her if it were true that her brother made Lee J. Cobb audition for Willy Loman. She said that it was. "Arthur never saw Willy as a big man. He always thought of him as a little man." My immediate thought was, "Doesn't Mr. Miller know what this play is about! Doesn't he realize that if a big man can't be a success in this country, then the American system is truly doomed!"

Obviously, Lee J. Cobb would pretty much define that part. Miller insisted that he hears the characters in his head when he writes. That's how he knows what actors will be able to play his characters. Later, what Miller realized about Lee J. Cobb was that "he had enormous straight-out power. He had anger that had real size, it wasn't a pipsqueak complaint. It was a profound insult that he had felt in life" (interview with Arthur Miller from *The New Yorker*, March 1, 2012). Cobb clearly brought something to the play that Mr. Miller had not seen.

I have seen numerous productions of *Death of a Salesman* and I hope to direct it someday. What I have come to understand is that each actor brings his own personal contribution to this part. It's true of any part. The actor's signature on the part of Willie Loman has to do with his understanding of life. "What the audience responds to is what is inside the actor." Jeffrey DeMunn was extraordinary in a production in San Diego. Completely different, but equally as powerful was Stacy Keach in a reading I saw in Los Angeles. Your life experience (and talent, of course) is going to make both your interpretation and your road into a play different from someone else's and different from the playwright's. You have an obligation to be true to the author's intent, but your road into it will certainly be your own. And with that you bring your insights into your character's relationship to the world of the play and the author's theme.

I've had a really interesting experience recently. My former student from New York University, Walker Vreeland, wrote a one-man show which is being performed in New York and around the country. It's a funny, tragic, personal story of his descent into the hell of mental illness and his recovery. What's made it particularly interesting is how differently I approach his acting and any editing to the script that needs to be done. The impulse that made him write it is a different muscle from the tools he must access in order to play it. I actually found myself saying, "What the writer is doing here is . . ." and often Walker has been completely surprised at what he's written. He was surprised at what it meant.

My friend the late James McLure wrote a play called *Lone Star*. The play opens with Roy looking at the stars behind a bar. "Star bright,

Star light," he says. When Conan McCarty did this opening in Stella Adler's scene study class, she stopped him to point out, "When a character is looking at the stars, he's not happy with his life on earth and is looking to go someplace else." When I told McLure this, he said, "My God. That's brilliant. I'd never thought of that."

What makes it difficult for us is that we have to both figure out what the writer is trying to say—and then find our own road in to get there, through the world of the characters that we've been given. I suppose it's an interesting snobbery that we know more than the playwright.

The Difference between a Plot and Justification

Dear Milton,

In terms of the exercise that we are working on, how can you distinguish between adding a plot—and finding an impulse or justification for moving onstage? I am struggling with that.

Dear Theresa,

Like all of the elements of the technique of acting, they overlap and they affect each other. It's understandable there would be some confusion.

Although I have become a broken record when it comes to saying, "You're building a plot," it's not that you shouldn't use a plot—or that it doesn't exist. Plot is everywhere. It's essential. You can't have a character without a plot. After all, the way a character responds to a plot (among many other things) tells us who they are. You cannot have a past without a plot. Your character in *Fifth of July* was raised by Sally and Matt. That's part of the plot of the play, and Shirley's past affects who she is now. Even the Talley place has a plot connected to it. It's been in the family for generations (as well as in two other plays). Sally wants to bury Matt's ashes there. Ken wants to sell the place. All of these elements are plot.

Every play has a multitude of facts. Plot is part of this "multitude of facts." Because a major responsibility of the actor is to make the facts of the play believable and to achieve the *experience of the facts*, you don't want to bog yourself down with a bunch of other plot points that you must also earn, and that don't actually feed into your play. In other words, there is a plot that exists in a play—and you must make it believable. While it's true you will use other plots to do this, you have to take on board that all of these other plots also have to be made believable. The fact that you say it doesn't make it true.

The simplest example of the use and abuse of plots is the "imaginary vacation" exercise we do. Joanne went snowboarding in New Zealand, but what she added was a long collection of plot points about getting a call from Lupita who was exhausted and dying for an adventure. Then they threw a dart at a map and ended up in New Zealand and they were able to get a cheap flight. On and on and on. The problem is that you must build all of those elements believably, otherwise you're just throwing out nonsense. When poor Maurizio built his vacation, he got so bogged down in ticket prices and changing planes and who to go with and choosing a hotel that he never made it to New Zealand at all.

There is no question you could use all of these plot points and make them feed you, but the problem with both Joanne and Maurizio is that their plots became a complicated grocery list and not a fascinating experience.

Justification is different. It's really the "why" of acting. And the rule for justification is that it must ignite your talent. If I ask you, "Why did you go snowboarding in New Zealand," the answer is not the plot. "Well, I was exhausted and I needed to get out of the country and I knew that Lupita liked snowboarding." The why behind all of it might be something like, "I needed to nourish my soul." Or "to piss off my ex-lover." Or "to kill my boredom." Whatever. And, yes, I need to build what needed nourishing, or having an ex-lover, or my boredom . . . but I'm now drowning in plot that isn't feeding me. Not that it can't feed me, but neither plot that Joanne or Maurizio chose gave them anything but frustration.

That's the reason I make such a big deal about the tendency to throw in extraneous plots. You absolutely must earn every word you say as an actor and the mere fact you utter the words doesn't make it true. Granted, if you have enough talent, you can make anything believable, but you want to be selective in your choices. That's what bogged Maurizio down. Building too many plots is a classic tendency, but I find these plot stories are both uninteresting and not really relevant or necessary to the play. It's really important your choices kick butt. Really excite you. Otherwise you get bogged down in a mess of stuff that doesn't feed the play and it's boring you and everyone else to death.

Stella: "If you're bored with your choice, the audience will be bored."

In the justification exercise we're doing at the moment, we have a garage and ten things to do in it. We're exploring **justification** as a concept. The simplest definition of justification is "why?" "Why" am I doing the ten things I have been asked to do? The first question I would ask is, "Why am I going into the garage?" If I were doing the exercise, I would no doubt add a plot here. And this is where it gets dangerous. I want a plot that feeds me, but also a plot I can make believable.

Some plots, some justifications take more work than others. With work I can make the fact that I live in Lebanon, Missouri, believable. In the same way I can make the Castle at Elsinore believable. But I have to do the work. If you look back on the exercises we've had this year, among them: visualizing, living in the place, connecting to what you're talking about. All of these come into play with this.

Let's go back to the plot of why I'm going into the garage: I might choose, "There's a wardrobe in the corner of the garage that is magical and it leads to a mythical country called Narnia." Or maybe, "The garage belonged to Stella Adler and there's a box in it where she kept the secret of acting." Any of these are possible, *as long as I can believe them and I do the work to earn them*. And, never forget, your choices must bring you to life. "My grandmother told me there was a broken lightbulb in her garage and she wanted me to go fix it," not only doesn't feed me, I have to build a grandmother, where we were when she told me, if she told me in the kitchen—then I have to build the kitchen, etc. A plot can really bog you down rather than pump you up.

The second part of your confusion has to do with the use of the word "impulse."

The impulse is not so far removed from the plot or the justification, but I think of it as a more accessible vocabulary word. If I were to see an actor standing offstage, about to go on, and I asked, "What's your action?" I can only imagine the frozen look I would get. If I ask, "Why are you going out there?" I have a much better chance of stimulating an actor. I think of it as an impulse that takes me out there. But, listen, don't let the vocabulary words confuse you. They're not that important. Your entrance as Shirley in *Fifth of July* was "to show myself" or "to thrill them with the fabulousness of me." Whether it was an impulse or a plot doesn't really matter that much. It was active, it stimulated you. What it really is, is an *action*, but it's another word that is not so important. Forget the word "impulse" if it messes you up. It's not important. There's something that makes you go into the room. The *something* might easily be, "He'll kill me when he finds out I'm here." Call it what you want. It's playable. It brings me to life.

Justification is useful for all of your movements in the space. You will find it useful to talk it out. To have a running dialogue to stimulate your movement. If you talk it out, you'll be able to clearly figure out if it's feeding you or not. Talking it out doesn't mean reporting it in a dry tone, which can easily sound like a blow-by-blow description of what I'm doing. As long as you make every step along the way truthful and it's affecting you, then you'll be on the right track. Also, don't get literary when you talk things out. You're an actor, not a writer. "What a dusty box" is hardly great writing, it's hardly writing . . . but in the hands of the right actor it can have about it the excitement of adventure and the thrill of anticipation. It's your connection to what you say that you're after.

I cannot emphasize enough "the way you say it is the way you'll do it." If you recite or report, "There's the box," then you're going to be dead in the water. If you force it and say with mock enthusiasm and your face all twisted up, "THERE'S THE BOX!!!" then you'll still be dead in the water. And I will scream along with everyone else, "Lies!" Don't rush. Don't rush to performance. Don't rush your choices. Let the object tell you what you need. It may take a while, but the more you exercise this, the easier it becomes.

What we call it doesn't matter. There's a reason I go to the box. It doesn't matter what I call it. No one is going to test you on this. If you're not careful the vocabulary of acting will cripple you. Define the terms however you like. The point is when you look in the box, you want to be brought to life and you will bring us with you.

Stella Adler had a cousin who taught our class once a week. Pearl. She was a total delight as a person, and you could always feel her personal investment in everything. I was sitting in the school office one day when Pearl walked in. She asked me if we had a "lost and found." I didn't know. She then explained. "Someone has lost a glove." There was a brief pause as she presented the glove to me and then studied it. "It's an *old* glove." Yet another pause. Her focus and concentration getting ever stronger. And then, as if King Lear were describing the heath she said, "It's an *old, dirty brown glove.* (a theatrical pause) And someone has lost it." I wanted to applaud.

Sit Down, You're Not the Audience!

In order for you to have this great privilege to live in a world full of imagination, you need an aliveness that is different from the outside world.

—Stella Adler

Develop a sense of what is good theater. This is a rough one, but it's a skill that comes with experience. One of the ways to help yourself is to begin to identify why you like or do not like a play or a performance. It's important as an actor that you don't allow yourself to have a mindless opinion. "I loved that," "I hated that," "I think he's brilliant"—But why? You have to strive to achieve an educated opinion.

Class discussions about plays or films and sometimes television shows often sound like a group of fans sitting around a coffee shop. "Oh, I loved that!" "I can't stand her." "Boy has he aged!" Or the obligatory standing ovation at the end of every performance that happens in America—from a high school musical to Broadway.

Dear Kevin,

You need to stop thinking of yourself as a member of the audience. If you're an actor, you no longer can sit in the audience and demand to be entertained. You must develop a critical eye for the theater. When you watch a play, you are no longer allowed to say, "Oh, I loved that" without saying why. What specifically did you love about it? And then you can begin to evaluate your reasons as being either those of an artist in our work—or part of the crowd. As an actor, it's part of your job to be intelligent about what your colleagues do. You cannot sit back and say, "Show me!"

When Teo and I left the Donald Margulies play the other afternoon, he immediately talked about what was wrong with the performances. "The actors had no past. No one was living in the circumstances of the play. Not one fact was earned." That's an actor talking, not an audience member. Also, it didn't matter that the production was unsuccessful, or as my friend David said to me recently, "I wanted my two hours back." For Teo, it became a learning experience.

As an actor you must include the audience. They are part of the theater experience. They are your partners in the experience. But you are not allowed to be one of them. My friend, Patrick, is an amazing tennis player. I am not. I am an audience. I told him recently how much I liked watching Rafael Nadal. He was able to explain to me in extraordinary detail the strength of Mr. Nadal. As an actor, you must know what other actors are doing and be able to explain in the same detail what you see and precisely why it does or doesn't work.

Mind you, I still believe the audience is the lowest common denominator of human existence. Don't trust them. And certainly don't be one of them. If they give you a standing ovation, it's not because they have great taste. It's probably because they're reaching for cellphones that are stuck in their pockets.

An actor in Stella's class once stopped in the middle of a monologue and said, "I'm sorry Stella. I got nervous." Stella with a compassion she often lacked, assured him, "Of course, you're nervous. You go out every night and expose your nerve endings . . . your soul . . . your life work to people who sit back and judge you. And you thank them for the opportunity to be there. It's the greatest nobility."

How Do You Rehearse When There's No Rehearsal?

In my advanced scene study class the other day, I had everyone read a short scene—everyone reading the same scene. Not out loud. I then asked them what hit them first. They were all different. A couple of the actors were in the same ball park, but for the most part, everyone was hit by something different. Considering how much work is done away from the actual rehearsal room, you really have to keep open to your own process.

From Greg: As actors, we have many variables to juggle on stage. For me, it has always been things such as actions, personalization, posture, breath support, diction, stakes, listening to my scene partner, and visualization. I have always said to myself that if I focus on just one thing each rehearsal, then it will all come together.

Dear Greg,

I think only working on one thing at a time is problematic. Eventually you need to trust your talent and let it go where it wants. It's way too restrictive for me to decide to only work on one thing at a time.

At the college I fight with people all the time about having to turn in a lesson plan. What do they expect me to do when someone asks me about character? Answer with: "I'm sorry, but we don't get to that until the third week of next semester." When you're rehearsing you have to allow yourself to say, "Hm. I wonder why he's doing that?" And then go down that road. You'll cut off all kinds of creative impulses if you stop yourself, "No. I don't get to the relationship they had in college until tomorrow." To only work on one thing makes no sense. It's like saying, "I'm only going to work on the backhand during this practice session. If someone hits me a forehand, I'll ignore it."

Truly building the world of the play as it occurs to you, step-by-step, allowing the play to gestate—to simmer—in your inner being, so to speak . . . it allows you to morph into the characters' consciousness. How they think. How they see the world. Trust yourself. And sure, you'll go down the wrong road periodically, but that's the joy of acting. Rehearsals are not like life. If you go down the wrong road in life, it could be a disaster. If you go down the wrong road during rehearsals, you can stop and say, "Well . . . that didn't work"—and try something else.

I would also add that working on one thing at a time can easily lead you to setting in cement your actor choices, rather than letting them change and grow as your understanding of the part grows. I see you doing that in exercises we're working on in class at the moment. You decided on something you wanted to use and you got stuck, because you wouldn't give it up. Maybe one of the biggest lessons we have to learn is to trust our impulses. And, also, I would just point out that if you make a mistake, you won't die.

More from Greg: Additionally, in Good, *you would often compare moments in a scene with something from real life. For instance, when you were trying to get me to understand the attitude of the clerk to the people coming into the building, you said to me, "The Clerk is like the guard in public safety . . . " The relation helped me get a better idea of how a certain situation in a scene is similar to something we understand without bringing it down to our level. I found that to be effective without having to think of my dog dying.*

I think this is how we carefully get to the *nature* of the given circumstances in a play—including all sorts of stuff: relationships, actions, the plot, on and on and on. It's a dangerous area, granted. You have to understand what's going on and then leave it and go back to the play.

In *Good*, Maurice wanted train tickets so he could leave Nazi Germany and since Halder, his close friend, was in the SS, it made sense he could get them. Obviously, you can't substitute wanting to leave Germany with wanting a job at NBC, but what is clear about the similarity is that it doesn't make sense that if my friend knew I was qualified for the position, he wouldn't do something to make it possible. Like give me the job. In Maurice's mind, Halder wants him to be safe and he has the power to do something . . . so why doesn't he. It has to do with the nature of friendship with a person in power.

More Greg: I am just trying to find the gray area between what I am currently learning and what I have learned in the past. If I find similarities, great—it helps to strengthen the belief. If something proves to be unhelpful, then I abandon it.

There is no reason to spend a lot of time trying to see whether something you've learned in the past works. There are no absolutes in acting. Trying to analyze something like that puts way too much emphasis on the academics of acting. Also, what works for one part won't necessarily work for another. I was reminded recently of what I consider an absurd example of actor teaching. There are actors who will listen to their iPods before a scene or an audition. I've never liked it because it forces you into a mood, but I decided to be more open so when I saw an actor doing it, I thought, "Well, if it works, who am I to say anything?" It didn't work. His audition was less than inspired. On the other hand, Marlo Thomas did it before filming scenes in a television movie I produced. She won an Emmy Award for the performance. My point is, you must find what works for you, based on trying and possibly failing. Don't get stuck in your books. An added note: please don't try listening to music on an iPod before a scene or entrance. It will force you into playing a mood—or it will disconnect you from the play. Marlo could get away with it, but I've never found that to be true for anyone else.

Also, you have to take on board your growth as an actor. When Petrovski started out, he always had to ask himself, "What happened before this scene?" Now, he takes it in automatically. It's the reason I always have doubts about actors teaching acting. There are certain things you do that become second nature and you forget you ever had to approach them as a part of a process.

There are numerous roads into your talent. It's completely tongue-in-cheek when I call your previous training "bad training." What bothers me is that teachers believe there is only one way to do something. Their way. And they don't see when their methodology is crippling an actor. Colin is so in his head he gets stuck. Frozen. And yet at the other school, they had him write fifty pages of backstory. No wonder he's in his head. Makes no sense to me at all.

You will have rehearsed at home, in the car, around the theater . . . wherever. You make certain choices. You explore them. You work to experience them. And then when you arrive at rehearsal you have to forget your homework, certainly don't attempt to *show* what you worked on . . . and see what happens. It's a big step to trust that your work is always "in" you and that it takes on another life . . . a new life, once you get on your feet. Keep in mind the most exciting acting happens when you're willing to fly without a net. But think how much you have to know before you're willing to say, "Take away the net!"

A Little Venting, if You Please

There are numerous emails I receive from actors who have studied other ways of working and are now trying to figure out the answer. Acting teachers probably should have some kind of Hippocratic Oath, where they agree not to be so damned adamant about *their* method. In 1931 the famous American director Josh Logan met Stanislavsky and asked him to define certain terms being used by American actors. Stanislavsky immediately stopped him. "That's for Russians. We're different than Americans. You must come up with your own method."

I would add to my list of actor sins the idea that actors ask about concepts they've never tried. They want to know what the theory means without having tried it.

10
Rehearsals

Notes for a First Rehearsal

To the cast of *Good*, by C. P. Taylor. (*Good* is a play exploring how a good man in Germany in the 1930s becomes a Nazi.)

Since most of you haven't worked with me before, I'll explain a bit how I approach working on a play.

Writers write plays because they have something to say. Something they believe. Something that angers them. Something they are reflecting. Whatever the reason . . . writing is their way of saying it. Obviously, for the actor, our way of communicating ideas is different. We say what we have to say through the human beings we are playing. We are a vessel for the themes of the author.

A character does not know that they're a theme, but as an actor you do. And knowing what the play is about thematically informs the choices you make. It's the actor's way of contributing to the text. So I would say an early goal of ours—and not necessarily one that is easily discovered—is: "What is the writer trying to say?" If I, as an actor, connect with what the writer is trying to say, and by that I don't necessarily mean I *agree* with my character's point of view, but I personally connect to this idea, then the audience will respond. I like the idea of saying in a sentence or two, "Why should we do this play?" We'll make a note to ourselves to get to this in the next month.

Your personal relationship (you . . . the actor) to the theme of the play is what the audience responds to. In other words, if you personally understand what you're talking about . . . what the theme is, the audience will get it. It kind of goes back to my first exercise in Technique Class: something I love and something I hate. If the actor loves something, then the audience will love it. If you hate it, then the audience will hate it. If the actor who is *for* something and the actor who is *against* it are equally strong, then the audience will understand the impossibility of the world we live in. There are no right answers. And, if you include the audience, they will thank you for it.

Hopefully this will explain why we spend time on the meaning of the play. You must be able to figure out how your character fits into what the writer is trying to say.

It's important to understand the road to get to what the writer is trying to say requires enormous depth. From you the actor. Great plays are plays with big ideas and the joy of acting is we grow as people because we stretch ourselves up to the size of the idea.

To get to this depth, we start with the WORLD OF THE PLAY. The writer has given us a world to live in and the play comes out of that world. That's what we're doing now. We are exploring the world of *Good*. Germany in the 1930s. The more we understand about the world of the play, the more easily we will get to the big question of the characters: how do they deal (or not deal) with this world? Realism, which is the form we're in, was defined by Stella as: an ordinary man in extraordinary problems of the soul. The word "soul" gives you a sense of how deep this character problem . . . this *human being* problem . . . exists in a play.

Fight the urge to make decisions right away. Just let all of this information swim around in your being. The great Southern writer William Faulkner described this period of discovery as the Ingestion Period, which is followed by the Gestation Period. You ingest all this information; you take it in. And then you let it gestate. Let it simmer for a while.

If you don't rush this period, and certainly don't rush to performance choices, then the play will begin to open up for you. You can begin to daydream your character in this world you're creating. See them in various scenarios that the play leads you to. At some point you (the actor) will want to start asking your character questions. That is a great beginning of creative work, letting the facts of the play lead you to thinking. You don't have to answer the questions right away, but it gives you a road in. As your depth of understanding during the rehearsal period begins to broaden, there are questions you will go back to time and time again.

I would think every character in this play would want to explore how they felt when they first heard Hitler speak. Or maybe your character never actually heard Hitler speak, but you heard about it. Don't be overly structured with your questions. Feel free to simply wonder what your character must have thought. "I wonder what Maurice must have thought when someone told him about Hitler." Don't feel as if you have to answer the question right away, just because you came up with it. It's something you have to get to in time. The more experienced you get, the more you will begin to figure out what questions you can answer now and what questions will have to wait until you know more.

On an acting note: there are teachers who insist you always refer to your character as "I." I would hold off on that until you're comfortable. I have always found if you rush to refer to your character in the first person too early, you know you are lying and, as Stella Adler used to say, "If you lie on stage, it should hurt." Rushing anything connected to performance is going to make you uncomfortable, because you're lying and it doesn't feel right. I would use the third person until you're comfortable using the first person.

When you discover your character . . . and it starts you asking more and more questions, let it happen. Embrace it. Don't let it panic you. This is the joy of acting. One thing leads to another.

Take your time. Watch the documentaries. Read the script. Spend time without distractions. Let the visual images begin to feed you. Begin to see yourself in those streets. Don't push for performance choices yet. You need a lot more information before you start thinking about "how do I play this character?"

Trust your talent. Trust that all of the endless pieces of the puzzle will eventually fall into place and you will have a solid basis of performance. I hate puzzles, but I'm guessing it's a good metaphor. You get a box that assures you there are a thousand pieces. You throw them all out on the floor and out of all of these seemingly disconnected pieces, there suddenly appears two pieces that fit together. And then eventually another piece fits, maybe not with the two you have . . . but in another section. And then finally, something you've always wanted: the Eiffel Tower in the middle of your living room floor.

We have been given an enormous gift. We have time to solidly work on this play. Please spend countless hours outside of rehearsal so the rehearsals are productive. The creative process is extremely fragile. You have no idea where a piece of information comes from that is exactly what you were looking for. It's so damned exciting.

It's a Rehearsal, Not a Performance—Notes after a Second Rehearsal

The rehearsal process is of vital importance. And when you have a long rehearsal period, it's vital that rehearsals are not performances. Most experienced directors are aware of this and honor the actor's process. The actors at an early rehearsal of the Donald Margulies play *Time Stands Still* decided it was time to perform.

To the cast of *Time Stands Still*:

The characters are living on the surface at the moment. Your initial impulses were right on, but you haven't moved on from that impulse and you're not digging deeper. And because we're missing the underbelly of these character's lives, we're not getting to the play.

There is a uniqueness about the modern play in terms of character. Our search is: what is the character's inside? Modern theater deals with depth of character. There are no standard patterns in the Modern theater. There is no such thing as, say, "the good wife" or "the bad mistress." There is an inner struggle. There is an inner struggle within human beings and the plays, since the end of the nineteenth century, have reflected this. They have since Ibsen, Strindberg, and Chekhov.

Acting is not just a matter of making your dialogue sound believable and make sense. I applaud the fact you sound like humans, since way too often actors sound like they're "acting," but that's not all there is to it.

As actors we cause ourselves problems because we go to the lines too quickly. I even think read-throughs are dangerous, since they move us subtly into character choices, line reading choices, performance choices . . . all without an informed basis for our decisions. In order for us to figure out what is going on, we have to dig and question and look deeply into the text. And, until it becomes a habit, you have to consciously make this effort. *Time Stands Still* is an extraordinary exercise in acting. If you only go to the lines, you will think much of the play is the action "to chat." When you go deeper, you get to overwhelming human struggle.

One of the places we can go is to think clearly about what these people have been through before the play starts. That past walks in with each of them.

You must always have a pre-existing past for the character. I cannot say enough or emphasize enough the importance of *experiencing* this past. Fight like hell that dead tone of analyzing or reporting. It's not enough just to say he was worried about her. What does "worried" mean? In depth! Give it life or death proportions. You can't play it as if you're worried she got stuck in traffic. She was in a war zone in a Jeep that was bombed. A fellow worker was killed, and it could have been her. What you bring to the circumstance of the play is the character's continuation.

Another key: don't take on too much at once. Just take on what you can believe. One thing at a time. If you start to build "he's a journalist," "he left the war zone early," "he almost died from a bomb blast," "as soon as he got the phone call, he was on the next plane to Germany," . . . if you build them all at the same time, you'll have a nervous breakdown.

The play is there to prove the past. In other words, there is a past that exists—and then we have this play. The play already exists before James says from offstage, "Almost there . . ." and Sarah says, "I see." It's not about telling her where the apartment is. They've lived there for eight years, she obviously knows where the apartment is. In the same way when Richard enters and says, "Heyyyy!" There's a past in existence. We have to own this past. If behind "heyyyy!" isn't the sense of how close she came to dying, then it's a play about saying "hello."

Assignment for tomorrow's rehearsal: a one-minute monologue (roughly) that gives you an impulse for scene 2. Please remember this is only a rehearsal. You are experimenting with a concept. The idea here is not "to get it right." It is to begin to play with your technique and see how it helps you. Speak as the character (always!). Don't explain why you've made the choice you've made. Just do it. I would expect you might rehearse your choice at home—and when you arrive at rehearsal, allow your choice to grow and be different.

One Rehearsal Does Not a Performance Make

The need to make it all work immediately can really stifle you in rehearsals of a play. The security of having a group of people develop an understanding together is truly invigorating, but I'm aware that having everyone working at a different pace and with a different focus can be frustrating.

Dear Cast,

Noah brought up a salient point yesterday after rehearsal: there was no relationship between Halder and Maurice. It was an overstatement, of course, but certainly there was not the relationship we expect to get to before we invite an audience. But, it was the first rehearsal.

It's vital you begin to understand that a week and a half of script analysis does not mean you will be able to pick up the script and turn in a performance. You may be able to do this with a television script, but not with a play that has any depth. Certainly it is good to be aware what is missing, but it's also important to not think it's a failure on your part. What did exist was monumentally important for a first read: a clear sense of what the two of you were talking about. And even though you were stuck with the script—and kept having to look down—there was still a sense that you were responding to each other. Not as much as you eventually will, but there was a vital layer where the semblance of a scene existed. Surprisingly enough—and a tribute to both of you—as you worked through the scene you allowed impulses to hit you and you acted on them.

All of you, please don't demand of yourselves a performance on day one. How about not even on day ten. Give yourself permission to believe what you can believe today, knowing you will believe more tomorrow. Be clear what you're trying to accomplish, then improvise the scene, then discuss what happened based on what you were working on, and then do the scene again. I encourage all of you to work this way when you're rehearsing outside of our scheduled rehearsals. If you will develop this habit, it will become the way you work and you will never again just mindlessly throw yourself blindly into the fray with hopes that something will land. Sometimes I feel as if there's a little bit too much wandering around, hoping you'll bump into your destiny.

One of my first jobs involved being at rehearsals for a production of *King Lear* at Lincoln Center. Jerry Freedman was the director and during a rehearsal one of the actresses playing one of the daughters turned to Jerry and asked, "Is that what you want?" His response was quite simple: "If you're asking me if you're going in the right direction, the answer is 'yes.' If you're asking me, 'is this what I want opening night?' absolutely not." It's the reason I forbid you to say to me, "but yesterday in rehearsal you said." *Yesterday* we didn't know as much as we know today.

Giving yourself to the rehearsal and letting your work go where it may is essential. I realize it's a huge leap to trust your work is "in you," but if you're not careful you will try to "play" your homework. If you get used to the idea of giving yourself totally to the rehearsal process, it will allow you to surprise yourself. It's quite phenomenal how much of the homework stays with you.

A year after the above email, one of the actors was in my production of Dis-graced. *He was still struggling with this idea.*

> I know it's extremely difficult to let go of the work you've done outside of rehearsal and trust that it's there, but you and Tyler were both so determined to play your choices, you might as well have been in different rooms. Listen to each other and respond to what's going on in the scene. Your choices will still be there, but they will be enhanced by allowing another element into the mix.
>
> You need to be open to the idea that your creative work opens you up to numerous possibilities. And you must let it. Let's say you're working on Abe and why he dresses like an American, which might make you wonder what he thinks about Amir and Emily's apartment. Don't stop yourself from considering that, just because you were working on how he dresses. Don't sit on an impulse. That's part of the creative process. One thing leads to another.

To the Cast of *Destiny of Me*: Terrible Work Today! Just Terrible!

When we were in college we were advised to spend two hours outside of class for every hour in class. I'm guessing my friend Mickey did that and that's why he got into Harvard. Rehearsals are similar. And, for some reason actors believe the work they do in rehearsals is done and now they can wait until the next rehearsal to work again. This email was to the cast of the Larry Kramer play *The Destiny of Me* after a particularly deadly rehearsal.

> Dear Cast,
>
> Aside from Jean, none of you seem to have looked at the script between yesterday's rehearsal and today's.

There are facts in every play . . . countless facts. Although you will not be able to earn the experience of every fact in a play, part of your talent is figuring out which ones are essential to your performance. If the play says, "I went to Yale" . . . and you don't even know what Yale looks like, much less what it means . . . the *experience* of Yale . . . then you're a dime-a-dozen actor who gets by reciting lines as if they make sense.

What is not a dime a dozen is the actor who owns the experience of everything he talks about. If the play says, "I read a play called *Holiday*" and you don't know what that is, you're just a person on the street spouting empty words. If you are a doctor doing medical research and you don't know what that means during an AIDS crisis—has anyone watched *And the Band Played On*?—then you're approximating your limited idea of what it might mean. Based on what, I'm not sure.

And there is no excuse for this. You're living in a world where Google has done most of your work for you. Yet the laziness is overwhelming. I can't imagine what you would have done, back in the days when we had to lick postage stamps and go to a physical building, called *the library*. The American theater would have died between Monday and Tuesday.

At this point, Teddy and I have given you a skeleton outline. It is your job to fill this in with muscle, blood, and flesh. We cannot do this for you. If you look at all of the facts of the play, you will be overwhelmed. All of these facts must be fed through your imagination to become the experience of the facts. Otherwise there is no play. I would not be surprised to find out that no one has really worked on where you are in any given scene. What the house or the neighborhood looks like in Eden Heights. What the furniture is like in the dining room.

You have all done imagination exercises in Tim's class. You know how to use it. Apply it. Technique exercises are there to be applied, much like countless hours working on a backhand or shooting baskets or (God forbid!) hitting balls at a driving range . . . it's all in service of the production. Doing a play this early in your actor study is meant to help you bridge the gap between your technique classes and your performance abilities. But the work is on your shoulders. By now you should have discovered that an intelligent performance of the lines of a play is not going to give you acting. It just feels like a room full of liars.

A true actor is one who sits at a bar with a group of friends and thinks, "This is such a waste of time. I could be home working on my acting." And in this instance, you could be home working on countless things that have to do with this script. When you get lost, we can help you. Nothing pleases me more than an email from one of you asking for help because of a confusion. A confusion borne out of having worked on the script. Not borne out of a need for me to tell you how to do it.

The future is truly in your hands. Both for this play—and for your future as an actor. Don't let this opportunity pass you by. As Diana Ross once said, "There's plenty of room at the top. It's only at the bottom that it's overcrowded."

Second Night Doldrums

There is a strange phenomenon that happens with the second performance and even the second take, where any success seems to drop out. The problem most of the time stems from the need to recreate "last night's success" or "the success of the first take." One of the ways to avoid this is building (out loud!) more moments from the past.

A note to the cast of *Time Stands Still*:

We really have to fight the urge to lock down anything in a play. It seems to me we are getting dangerously close to stopping any kind of creative work. Maria Callas said she treated every performance as just another rehearsal. Do that. Treat these performances as a rehearsal. Start to trust you have the play in you and flying without a net a little will only make it better.

I would say it's a good idea to always build one more thing in the past for every performance. Specific to the play, of course. Not just any old past. Keeping a play fresh is part of the actor's job. Always have something you're going to do tonight you haven't done before. Something different on your entrance, perhaps. Not huge. Small and controlled. Last night the first scene was loose, fun, and alive. And then the second scene hit, and I felt as if I was getting a retread of the night before. The email James sends Sarah was not specific. It was a line. When Jamie sent another one . . . well, I don't have to beat you all to death on this. *You must keep the play fresh and alive*. You need to always have something new to contribute. Richard's entrance and response to Jamie was exactly the same, as if it had been choreographed. Don't let anything throw you or anyone else off, but always contribute to what you've got.

We've got a couple more rehearsals before they evict us. Let's enjoy our time and use it to the fullest.

To the Cast of *Godot*: Notes after Opening Night

Good morning, gents—

For what it's worth, word of mouth is quite good on the play. This next stage of the play's development is the most elusive in all acting.

Unfortunately it's not something you can specifically set out to achieve . . . or set in motion. It just happens. Stella describes it as "letting the play happen, instead of making it happen."

I went with my dear friend, David Meyer, to hear the legendary English director Peter Brook. David had toured the world in Mr. Brook's legendary production of *A Midsummer Night's Dream* and we hung on every word he said. At one point he described the three stages of an actor and I found it quite interesting. I used the analysis after opening night of *Waiting for Godot*.

Impersonating: This stage is something you have moved well beyond. As American actors we are less prone to imitation than the Brits. This stage for us is more cautiously walking on eggshells as we move forward. For each of you it is different. It's a difficult stage. Wanting to rely on your partner, but not knowing enough about who you are to do that. I might add it's a difficult period to watch as a director. Blake was playing his action, Chris was playing his—and neither the twain would meet. When Matt and Alec arrived, it was like watching four different plays going on. And then one day, magically you all were in the same play. (No doubt because Mark Donnelly was coming to watch you. The sudden pressure of such an expert witness.)

Inhabiting: This is where we are. Wonderfully. You have all inhabited your characters and as Mr. Brook suggests, "Every good play senses the present that it's in." You have actively relaxed into the circumstances of the play. More and more I see that there's an active, specific reason you go out onto the stage—an impulse—and then you easily let the next thing happen, and with seemingly no effort the play moves forward. Vladimir comes out for a reason. Estragon is there, so there's a play. If he hadn't been there it would have been another play. If Vladimir hadn't appeared, Estragon would have been in a different play (as we saw in the rehearsal where Chris played with that damned boot for five minutes). Lucky and Pozzo would have continued their journey had they not run into Vladimir and Estragon. As an actor it's often a good idea to think in terms of "what do I expect to happen" — and then "what does happen and how do I respond to it." If what you expected to happen does happen, you respond one way. If it doesn't, you respond another. It helps keep entrances fresh. Stella: "Never come in the same way twice." Tweaking your entrance helps keep the play always new.

Incarnation: Mr. Brook suggests once in a generation someone achieves this. I think this is where we're headed with this play. It's a kind of immersion into the part and the world of the play. There is always a moment when you're on a tightrope. We see your life in the moment, not your preparation. You're flying without a net. In teaching I've experienced it a few times . . . I can only guess it comes from never settling into a play. There's always a search, always discovery.

No one at the school has ever seen acting like this. My Script Analysis class was shocked. They would mention a moment they loved, and I told them that it was something you had come up with. What you've done with this play, no director could do. It is your play. The four of you are so magical to watch together. It's the famous "what you get for free" — rarely! — in a production. Four actors who love being on stage together. The audience gets the benefit. They're strapped in securely for a very bumpy ride. I have been directing for almost thirty years, and it's the first production I've ever done where people were saying to me they couldn't wait to come see it again.

Hopefully that sonuvabitch Mr. Beckett is flying around the universe and will drop in to help us. Although, truth be told, I'm convinced we've shown him what he wrote.

Keep at it.

11
Final Thoughts

Locker Room Talk

We could learn a lot from sports teams. The coach gives a rousing speech, and everyone goes out to kick ass. On occasion, I wonder what actors are doing in the spare time that keeps them from not being prepared for rehearsals or class. What is it they do that is so fascinating that it keeps them from doing something that will help them with their careers.

> Dear Matteo,
>
> During the first Technique Class I took with Stella, she asked us to write her a letter. The letter was meant to read, "Dear Stella—These are my strengths. These are my weaknesses." She then advised us: "If you have weaknesses, you must work like Hercules to overcome them." Stella knew how difficult actor problems were to overcome. If you have an accent, get rid of it. If you are lazy, fight through it. If you're stiff, take a dance class. All of these are doable. They're solvable. Chris arrived in Los Angeles, having lived in New Zealand for eighteen years. He had the thickest New Zealand accent you've ever heard. It took him a year, but he got rid of it. He became so good at accents, he was hired to play a Russian in twenty-nine episodes of *Madam Secretary*. Brad, on the other hand, didn't get parts in numerous musicals—and he has a great voice—because he couldn't move. For some reason he never took dance classes. Many of our actor problems are bad habits. I slouch. My voice is squeaky. Fixable problems. The fact I didn't fix them is my fault, no one else's.

There are some very clear reasons actors are good . . . or merely functional. The reasons actors are great is even clearer. It's all about the work. If you take time off to do whatever it is actors do when they take time off, you won't have a career. It's as simple as that. I've always admired the Christians and their insistence: "Don't blame Jesus if you go to hell!" I've always wanted a bumper sticker for actors, "Don't blame me if you don't have a career." I'm telling you how to get one. You must approach every play, every scene, every exercise, every audition as if you're playing the finals at Wimbledon.

Email from Paul: Real sucky class. Even though I worked on the photo exercise with Milton it was torturous. I realize now that if the work hasn't been done, if you haven't paid a price for your choices it does not work.

My dear friend, this is such a fortunate discovery. Evan had the same discovery after he and I had worked on iChat before his class scene the other night. He told me that the scene went well. His reflection was, "Interesting what happens when you work."

For some reason, actors believe that they can just get up and do it without working at it. I think I've mentioned before Evan's realization in my class at Yale. "It's really pretty daunting if you do the work." I'm not sure why my sports metaphors never land on actors. Perhaps me and a sports metaphor don't belong in the same world. But I always wonder what would happen if a tennis player decided to wing it. One of the world's most famous pianists—now deceased—Vladimir Horowitz once said (to Stella), "If I don't practice for a day, I know it. If I don't practice for two days, my wife knows it. If I don't practice for three days, the public knows it."

Most actors, especially in Hollywood, go to the gym every day. Sometimes for longer than an hour. Once in a while I run into an actor who spends an hour a day outside of an acting class. My brilliant son, incidentally, spent no less than three hours outside of class for every hour he was in class. And don't get me started with Facebook. If 90 percent of the actors at school spent as much time on acting as they did on Facebook, they'd be stars. I have a fantasy that one day instead of philosophies of life listed on Facebook, there will be an acting discovery—actually, don't listen to me. That could really turn out to be a nightmare.

Can't Work on Acting, I Have an Event

I asked an actor why he was taking a casting director's workshop and he replied, "She casts a lot of things I'm right for." Chris did one many years ago and got the highest marks on everything. I saved the sheet and when the casting director was casting something he was perfect for, he sent the sheet along with his head shot. Never heard from her. I wouldn't mind the idea so much, if the reason for taking such a workshop was to have the experience of auditioning, but it's the belief in networking as a way to get work that feeds into this extremely unhealthy atmosphere about the profession.

Dear Mr. Donnelly,

I was mildly pissed off all week, reflecting on how annoying it is when actors are focused on the wrong thing. And then in this morning's *New York Times* (August 27, 2017), there was an editorial by Adam Grant called "Networking Is Overrated," with the highlighted phrase "Good news for young strivers: It's not really who you know. It's what you do." It's a brilliant opinion piece as Mr. Grant cites various examples of success stories, not based on someone pursuing a connection, but rather doing the work. "Accomplishing great things helps you develop a network." From George Lucas, who was hired by Francis Ford Coppola as a production assistant (not because of connections, but because of ability) to Justin Bieber, who taught himself to sing and play four instruments and then put a handful of videos on YouTube, to Sara Blakely, who sold fax machines by day for two-and-a-half years so she could build her prototype of footless pantyhose by night. All examples of people who would eventually be given a boost because Coppola, Usher, or Oprah became aware of them, but not because they schmoozed their way into a relationship. The work came first.

I had a student who was obsessed with learning about acting. He was weird, because he never really worried about the business. He has only, always, worried about learning how to act. His problems have always been in trying to understand concepts of acting, something he has realized will last him a lifetime—since you can never truly understand everything there is to know about acting. But, the point is, acting has been his focus. Not the business. Not networking. Not beating the system. Acting. And no matter what the project was— whether it was class or a friend's short film or a reading at some small theater—he approached it as if he were on Broadway. After several years of extremely concentrated study, he began to get work. He had a solid foundation.

The student was Mark Ruffalo, whom I first worked with when he was nineteen. Mark would not be "discovered" until he was twenty-nine, while doing an off-Broadway play. He was "discovered" by Kevin Huvane, one of the owners of CAA. Trust me, Mark never pursued CAA. Talk about something that would never have occurred to him. It was something he assumed was way out of his realm of possibilities. All he had been worried about was becoming a good actor.

The work . . . the work . . . the work! It is all about the work! For some reason actors are obsessed with examples of people who have careers without studying. *Good Will Hunting* becomes the idea of a shortcut to success. "Ben and Matt wrote their own movie and starred in it. I'll do the same thing." Even though it was over twenty years ago and we still talk about it—because it only happens every twenty years, but it gives actors something to focus on instead of the work. And, by the way, Ben and Matt were friends at Harvard—a school you could never get into without working your ass off your whole life.

I coach actors all the time who are deluded into believing they're going to get a part on a series that's going to change their lives, when they have no idea what they're doing. *Acting classes* or *actor coaching* are drop-in affairs. Something an actor does for a quick fix. But if I suggest we meet once a week and go through technique exercises, it's as if I suggested we get together and work on trigonometry.

Every audition is like playing at Wimbledon. I think I can hazard a guess: no tennis player would play any tournament without having practiced daily. No one would be shocked to find out that during a tournament Rafael Nadal practices for two hours on his day off. An article in today's *Times* is a series of interviews with kids who aspire to someday be professional tennis players. Fifteen-year-old Geanna Richard, when asked how frequently she played tennis, replied, "Seven days a week." Fourteen-year-old Nia the same. Twelve-year-olds Taye and Jaden, the same—seven days a week.

Once in a great while, I meet an actor who works on his or her craft every day. Mostly it's trying to figure out how to do that web series that will allow them to be discovered and then they can network their way into success. Or having a quick coaching session prior to a big audition, just trying to get the key to success and a series.

I have never read an article about someone who went to "an event," where they got a lead role in something because they networked their way into it. So please. Let me know if that works for you.

One Last Question—Daily Work

From Greg: The semester is over, but the work is only beginning. When the play came to a close the first thing I said to myself was, "What's next?" I realize when a play is over there is this hunger for an actor to keep going, because you do not want to lose the momentum on the work that you have been doing. On the last day of class you mentioned that it is imperative to continue working at your craft daily. There is no time to take a "break" from acting simply because it is "winter break." I have a few routines like voice, speech, reading aloud that I do daily. While these are all good and necessary, I know that I need to work my imagination and probably other things as well. I'd like to put in around an hour for actual acting exercises every day, that would be doable. I remember "build one thing you love and one thing you hate." I'd love some kind of list of what I might work on.

In 1978, Stella handed out a sheet to us, which sort of gave a list of exercises we'd covered that year (class was thirty weeks, incidentally, not fifteen). Try some of these:

Note from Stella regarding actor work: 1978

1. Read aloud every day for ten minutes. Start by standing five feet from the wall. Reach the wall with your voice. Increase the distance from the wall every day.

2. Read an essay, an editorial, an opinion piece. Be able to communicate the author's ideas to another person in your own words. Be aware of the sequence of thoughts.

3. Read a contemporary article or editorial with a point of view, and develop your own point of view.

4. Be able to defend both sides of a contemporary social issue.

5. Discuss an idea. Have a point of view.

6. Select ten things from nature. Describe them to a partner.

7. See different shades, textures of colors. Put the color on something and in a place.

8. See fast. Look at an area (a room, store counter, a park, etc.) to the count of ten. Describe what you saw.

9. Choose five big nouns (sun, rain) and find five things that each does—and where.

10. Make a list of things that catch your attention in life.

11. See a scene from everyday life and recognize its eternal quality.

12. Take on the body and sound of an animal.

13. Create imaginary circumstances. What do you do when you wake up there? What can you do if you're hot? Cold? Tired?

14. On a blank sheet of paper describe, by seeing it and pointing to the specifics, a still life scene from a historical period.

15. Create imaginary circumstances and be able to live in it alone for fifteen minutes.

16. Practice muscular memory exercises. Work on ½ and ½ exercises. Half real (a suitcase), half muscle memory (weight inside).

17. Practice physical controls. Practice accents and dialects.

18. Tell imaginary stories.

19. Work on justification: the reason why something activates you. Take an object: (a) I like it; (b) I hate it.
20. Discover the epic quality of a common object.
21. Recognize different types of conversation: (a) give and take, (b) traveling from what your partner says, (c) from subject matter, thoughts.
22. Practice smartening and complicating physical activities.
23. Create a character outside of you. See someone. From what I see I will create their entire life.
24. Create the past of a character in a moment of conflict.
25. Describe (a) a dark scene to someone and (b) a light scene to someone.
26. Be aware of the nature of things and circumstances.
27. Keep a journal.
28. Read plays.

Stella Adler's Letter to Me—Back Before Emails

"Back in the day" was a pain in the ass. How the hell did we ever live without emails? I was having a terrible time during rehearsals for a play. I was working in a theater in East Hampton, on Long Island—and Stella was teaching in California. I didn't want to bother her with a phone call, so I wrote to her, outlining the problems I was having.

I don't remember what I said in my letter to her, since we didn't make copies of anything, but I'm including in this book her letter to me. What hits me, looking at the date of her reply, I must have written her on my day off, a Friday—the 4th of July in 1980. Stella probably received my letter on the following Thursday, July 9, and answered it on Friday, the 10. It means I would have not received the letter until the following Wednesday, July 16. What a horror it must have been to be lost in rehearsals for twelve days.

July 10, 1980

Dear lovely, beloved Milton

    I got your letter and I'm rushing to answer
because I want you to have confidence in yourself
as an actor. The actor in you is beginning to feel
the birth pangs in acquiring the role during the rehearsal period and that is very normal. The work
you do at home is done and is in you. Don't worry
about it. The things you have chosen for your background work, with your imagination, they will give
you the confidence of rehearsal. Don't try to play
the background. Give yourself to the rehearsal.
Take from your partner; go to your partner. Communicate sometimes eye to eye and sometimes any way
that it happens, by looking down and by doing something. Leave yourself open to others at rehearsal.
Remember the rehearsal period is a new period. Acting is not ballet. It has in it a freedom and modern plays are a free-form. A certain spontaneity is
the main quest at rehearsal. Don't you set readings
ever. Let them come. Don't cater to the audiece or
the director. This is just a warning - in comedy
don't set the laughs! Not for you, anyway. If they
come it's fine but don't aim at them.
    What else should I say? You've taken what you

wanted out of the work with me. You are intelligent and understood that the craft was a means towards an end and it's the means which awakens the talent. Let it go where it wants. That's the impressive joy of just letting it happen instead of forcing it.

It's going to be alright. I hope the letter gets to you because I want you to feel secure in yourself.

Give my love to the trees, the grass, the potatoe fields, the night, the stars, the sea, to anybody you meet, to everything you look at...just tell them Stella sends her love. And especially to her friend, who is going to give a fine performance.

Love to you, darling,

Stella

Index

acting. *See specific topics*

Acting (Boleslavsky), 34

Actions (Caldarone), 135

actions, playing: active verb used for, 134–35; Adler on, 143; character problems and, 139–40; do versus say and, 134; entrances and, 135–36; on every line, 141–45; experience and, 145; flexibility in, 140–41, 145; impulse and, 144–45; not words, 133–41; plot and, 144; relationship and, 141–42; rush to, 137–38; within scenes, 143–44; thesaurus used in, 134–35; tips for, 135–36; what is really going on?, 133–34; wording actions and, 137

An Actor Prepares (Stanislavsky), 138

Adler, Stella: on actions, 143; on actor versus playwright contribution, 151–54; on appropriate behavior, 16; on articulate acting, 71; on boring choice, 156; Brando learning from, 65; on character exercise in real world, 94; on choice, 4, 40, 156; on craft, ix; on defictionalizing, 59; emotional recall impacting, xii–xiii; on entrances, 180; exercise list of, 186–88; on facts, 37, 110–11; failure and, xii; as genius, 14; given circumstances and, xiii; Goethe quoted by, 97; Horowitz and, 182; on learning, 90; letter to author from, 188–90; on life experience, 125; on listening, 69; *Lone Star* and, 154; on lying, 22; mentorship by, xiii; on nerves, 161; not everyone can act and, 34; nuclear power comment of, 95; on overcoming weaknesses, 181; on past and present, 108; on place, 60; on play as about something, 67; on process, 35; on rehearsal, 189; on relating to

character, 27, 74; on size of ideas, 83; Stanislavsky teaching, xii–xiii; on stealing material, 127; on stretching your size, 79; on talent, 4; talk it out exercise of, 20; theater as temple and, 77; theme and, 118; using one's own life and, 119; on visualization, 55; on words, 30, 31–32

"Adventures in the Screen Trade" (Goldman), 151

Affleck, Ben, 185

Akhtar, Ayad, 9–10, 29

All My Sons (Miller): facts and, 149; no resolution in, 84; past building and, 108–9; reporting and, 50; size of ideas of, 83

The American Clock (Miller), 88, 147

Angels in America (Kushner), 109

Anna Christie (O'Neill), 27

audience: actors as never part of, 159–61; connection and, 1, 2; as lowest common denominator, 161; theme and, 69

audition: music before, 164; network and, 183; talk it out and, 24

automatic writing, 24

Awake and Sing (Odets), 70

Babe, Thomas, 150

Bacharach, Burt, 96

Bacon, Kevin, 126

Bankhead, Tallulah, 91

Barkin, Ellen, 40

Baron, Jeff, 91

baseball exercise, 63–64

Beckett, Samuel, ix

Been So Long (Walker), 126

Beethoven, Ludwig van, 54–55

belief, from knowledge, 20

CPSIA information can be obtained
at www.ICGtesting.com
Printed in the USA
BVHW030500200921
616996BV00008B/1

9 781493 061259